AT HIS FEET

Five Practical Principles to
Help You Live Victoriously,
Every Day!

TAMMY TASSONE

WESTBOW
PRESS®
A DIVISION OF THOMAS NELSON
& ZONDERVAN

Copyright © 2018 Tammy Tassone.

All rights reserved. No part of this book may be used or reproduced by any means, graphic, electronic, or mechanical, including photocopying, recording, taping or by any information storage retrieval system without the written permission of the author except in the case of brief quotations embodied in critical articles and reviews.

Scripture taken from the New King James Version®. Copyright © 1982 by Thomas Nelson. Used by permission. All rights reserved.

WestBow Press books may be ordered through booksellers or by contacting:

WestBow Press
A Division of Thomas Nelson & Zondervan
1663 Liberty Drive
Bloomington, IN 47403
www.westbowpress.com
1 (866) 928-1240

Because of the dynamic nature of the Internet, any web addresses or links contained in this book may have changed since publication and may no longer be valid. The views expressed in this work are solely those of the author and do not necessarily reflect the views of the publisher, and the publisher hereby disclaims any responsibility for them.

Any people depicted in stock imagery provided by Getty Images are models, and such images are being used for illustrative purposes only. Certain stock imagery © Getty Images.

ISBN: 978-1-9736-4168-1 (sc)
ISBN: 978-1-9736-4169-8 (hc)
ISBN: 978-1-9736-4167-4 (e)

Library of Congress Control Number: 2018911729

Print information available on the last page.

WestBow Press rev. date: 10/19/2018

A few words need to be said.

To John, my husband, for giving me the space I needed to hide with my computer and a bible and leaving everything undone while I wrote and prayed through this book. And for believing in this project...and me.

To my children Alannah, Accalia, Andrew and Nolan. I love you more than words can say.

To all the women who have been a part of my journey. Hugs to each and every one of you. You know who you are.

Most of all to God; thank you for using my fingertips to type your message. Thank you for saving me. Thank you for loving me. Thank you for You.

CONTENTS

Introduction ix
Scriptures to Hold On to xiii
Prayer xvii

Principle 1: Dependence

Chapter 1   Yes, You Can 1
Chapter 2   What's in a Name? 7
Chapter 3   The Faith Story 18
Chapter 4   Identity Crisis 42
Chapter 5   Restoration 54
Chapter 6   Lead the Way 68
Chapter 7   Promises of God 73

Principles 2 and 3: Humility and Serving

Chapter 8   A Humble Heart 103
Chapter 9   Pride Rears Its Ugly Head 109
Chapter 10   To Serve, with Love 113

Principles 4 and 5: Gratitude and Worship

Chapter 11   Attitude of Gratitude 123
Chapter 12   Worship 138

INTRODUCTION

I am very happy to meet you. There are no coincidences (at least I don't think so), so the fact that you have this book in your hand is awesome. The format of this book is more like a conversation between you and me, what we might talk about if we were having a great cup of coffee—which happens to be one of my favourite things to do. This book is my story; it's *our* story and it is mostly what I have learned so far on my life's journey as a Christian woman. I have always believed that people are very similar; if I was going through something, chances were high that someone else was too. I want to share myself and my heart and more of God with you. I hope you enjoy, but more so, dear friend, I hope it helps. I believe this world is a beautiful place, but sometimes it's hard, and sometimes it's harder than hard. That means we have choices to make. May the words contained within help you make the best choices you can, so you can have the life you really dream of.

    The purpose of this book is to gain more insight into some of the things we can do to deepen our faith. It's also to give us more tools and better perspective to see where in our hearts and lives we can dig into our faith a little deeper. Okay, sometimes a lot deeper. In our relationship with Jesus, we never arrive; it's always a journey. Some of you are nodding your heads and saying, "Yup, it sure is." You know, because you've just been through something or are smack in the middle of it. I sometimes seem to go right from one mess to another. That translates as one *lesson* to another. There are always lessons to be learned, and sometimes it takes that fresh perspective or those new skills to get us to the next level. God can, and does, use everything, but we must allow Him to. And friend, He never disappoints!

We will all find ourselves at different places in our journey and our walk with God. I am not in any way saying I have it all together! On the contrary, this book is my "walking out" of problems, and junk, and struggle. He is faithful! He loves us even when we are unlovable, and that miracle is the reason I am here on this earth, free and growing in Him. Our journeys have no arrival date, just an action plan, so to speak. The plan is to walk it out in a way that gets us closer to Him and living way more victoriously than we ever thought possible! There will be times when we know exactly where we are and where we are headed on our journeys, but often we really don't know. We may wish we knew more. We want details, and more often than not we don't have them. We find ourselves asking, "Why, how, and really?" far too often. Friends, I can totally relate. Through this book I strongly suggest that the circumstances that keep us asking those questions provide the fertile ground for us to blossom and flourish through to the next level. The word *grow* is way too boring to describe what really happens as we dig in deeply with God. Growth automatically brings change, and God uses the layers of change to sanctify us.

Victorious living has always been my passion! I ache to see people, particularly women, living free, happy, and complete in God. There really should be something visibly different about us as Christ followers that lets others know we are His. I want to be that kind of example. When I live by these daily principles, life is amazing, separate from life's circumstances. I'm talking about the kind of peace that surpasses all understanding (sound familiar?), as well as blessing and fun and the best ride you could ever be on! Sometimes life can heap it on, but we have access to peace and guidance amid the yuckiest of stuff!

God's Word is full of stories that teach us. He also uses different kinds of people in His Word, so we all have someone we can relate to. One of the references from Scripture I would like to explore with you (and which is the basis for this book) is feet—specifically, stories of people at Jesus's feet. I would like to use these New Testament references to show you some of the life principles uncovered by these scriptures and the way to use these every day on our journeys to victorious living.

The ideas contained on these pages are referred to as "principles" because, well, they are. Principles are concepts and values that are guides for behaviour. You will be reading about depending on God, being humble, serving others, worshipping God, and being grateful. These core values are crucial to victory, which we all want, right? The absence of principles, on the other hand, being "unprincipled," would be considered a serious character defect. There is no way we can walk the Christian walk and be unprincipled at the same time. I would say that many people meet God through a time of unprincipled actions, but God ensures that He infuses us with new ones. That's what this book is about: newness.

We will be looking at the five principles and spending some time understanding how each one can get us back on track when we have lost our way and how each one can allow us to strengthen our relationship with Jesus. All we need to do is go to His feet and apply a simple principle. Jesus told us He is the way. The principles are easy to understand, not always easy to do. The body of Christ around us is filled with people we know who are living examples of what we will learn. I will share stories of people I know to bring it to life.

Walking out what we know is the goal here; it's the purpose of this book. We must use what we learn and put it to action. Remember, the point is to gain insight and tools to allow us to live (more) victoriously! It's God's dream for us. He wants us to be happy and whole all the days that we walk this earth. *"I have come that they may have life, and have it more abundantly"* (John 10:10).

The following scriptures form the foundation of this book. All come from the New Testament. All are from the NKJV (New King

James Version), my personal favourite. Together, these scriptures create the themes—or principles—of this book. Some of them work in unison, and a couple, just on their own, carry the weight of the information God wants us to have. Refer to them as often as you need to.

SCRIPTURES TO HOLD ON TO

Matthew 15:30
Then great multitudes came to him, having with them the lame, blind, mute, maimed and many others; and they laid them down at Jesus' feet and He healed them.

Matthew 28:9
And as they went to tell His disciples, behold, Jesus met them, saying "Rejoice!" So they came and held Him by the feet and worshipped Him.

Mark 7:24–25
And He entered a house and wanted no one to know it, but he could not be hidden. For a woman whose young daughter had an unclean spirit heard about Him, and she came and fell at His feet.

Luke 7:37–38
And behold, a woman in the city who was a sinner, when she knew that Jesus sat at the table in the Pharisee's house, brought an alabaster flask of fragrant oil, and stood at His feet behind Him weeping; and she began to wash His feet with her tears, and wiped them with the hair of her head; and she kissed His feet and anointed them with the fragrant oil.

Luke 8:26–29, 35
Then they sailed to the country of the Gadarenes, which is opposite Galilee. And when He stepped out on the land, there met Him a certain man from

the city who had demons for a long time. And he wore no clothes, nor did he live in house, but in the tombs. When he saw Jesus, he cried out, fell down before Him, and with a loud voice said, "What have I to do with you, Jesus, Son of the Most High God? I beg You, do not torment me" ... then they went out to see what had happened, and came to Jesus, and found the man from whom the demons had departed, sitting at the feet of Jesus, clothed and in his right mind.

Luke 10:38–39
Now it happened as they went that He entered a certain village; and a certain woman named Martha welcomed Him into her house. And she had a sister called Mary, who also sat at Jesus' feet and heard His word.

Luke 17:12–16
Then as He entered a certain village, there met Him ten men who were lepers, who stood afar off. And they lifted up their voices and said, "Jesus, Master, have mercy on us." So when he saw them He said to them, "Go, show yourselves to the priests." And so it was that as they went, they were cleansed. And one of them, when he saw that he was healed, returned, and with a loud voice glorified God, and fell down on his face at His feet, giving him thanks. And he was a Samaritan.

John 11:32
Then, when Mary came to where Jesus was, and saw Him, she fell down at His feet, saying to Him, "Lord, if you had been here my brother would not have died."

John 12:1–3
Then, six days before the Passover, Jesus came to Bethany, where Lazarus was who had been dead, whom He had raised from the dead. There they made Him a supper, and Martha served, but Lazarus was one of those who sat at the table with Him. Then Mary, took a pound of very costly oil of spikenard, anointed the feet of Jesus and wiped His feet with her hair. And the house filled with fragrance of the oil.

John 13:5, 12–16

After that, He poured water into a basin and began to wash the disciples' feet, and to wipe them with the towel with which He was girded....So when He had washed their feet, taken His garments, and sat down again, He said to them, "Do you know what I have done to you? You call Me Teacher and Lord, and you say well, for so I am. If I then, your Lord and Teacher, have washed your feet, you also ought to wash one another's feet. For I have given you an example, that you should do as I have done to you. Most assuredly, I say to you, a servant is not greater than his master; nor is he who is sent greater than he who sent him. If you know these things, blessed are you if you do them.

Mark 5:22-23/Luke 8:41-42

And behold, one of the rulers of the synagogue came, Jairus by name. And when he saw Him, he fell at His feet and begged Him earnestly, saying, "My little daughter lies at the point of death. Come and lay Your hands on her, that she may be healed, and she will live."

Luke 7:44–46

Then He turned to the woman and said to Simon, "Do you see this woman? I entered your house; you gave Me no water for My feet, but she has washed My feet with her tears and wiped them with the hair of her head. You gave Me no kiss, but this woman has not ceased to kiss My feet since the time I came in. You did not anoint My head with oil, but this woman has anointed my feet with fragrant oil.

PRAYER

Lord, may the message in this book bring You honour, and may it kindle a flame or light a fire in the hearts of those who read it. May we all be blessed by the hearing of, the learning of, and the studying of your living Word. In Jesus's name. Amen.

PRINCIPLE 1: DEPENDENCE

CHAPTER 1

Yes, You Can

DEPENDENCE. FOR MANY OF US, DEPENDING ON GOD IS a way of life. For others, daily dependence may seem like a stretch. Past hurts, current challenges, wrong identities, and simply not knowing *what* we can depend on Him for can prevent us from being successful in the way we would like—and ultimately the way we need. The throes of life can have us running from morning until night. Our demanding jobs, children, busy social schedules, volunteering, school activities, and so on can keep us going all day, day after day. I totally get this. My husband and I had four children within five years, with a set of twins among them. We are both entrepreneurs, and I am an only child with no family to help me out. The result is that we are very busy. I am way too busy for comfort most of the time. This concept is near and dear to my heart, because there is no way that I can do it all on my own strength—and honestly, I don't want to. I did for a long time, but finally I had the sense and humility to give it over. I did this much later than I should or could have; hence I learned how important it is. "If I knew then what I know now!" How many of you have said that? My hope is that some of you catch yourselves before you get burned out. God is so gracious, and He wants to help us. Psalm 37:23 says, *"The steps of a good man are ordered by the Lord, And He delights in his way."* Let's let Him. Let's get over ourselves, give up the control, and let Him help. You are wondering, *Then what?* We will discuss this in a later section. Just know that rest and peace in Him are so necessary and so possible.

Whether we are dependent believers or not so much, this chapter will allow us to identify what we can give over, what we can receive from Him, and how we can put it into daily living. Remember: *victorious living is the goal.* We are meant to be free and whole persons. Jesus came to save us from death and hell. But He also taught with passion how to live *this* life free and in Him. Being saved believers will get us into heaven, but we shouldn't have to wait until then to see the glory of God. He is here. He is ready. He is waiting and aching to have a deeper relationship with us, no matter where we are on this earth or where we are on our life journeys. There are no circumstances He cannot use as our starting points.

There are things that we as humans want to have or do. There are relationships we ache for, jobs we chase down, and attitudes that keep our hearts closed. Friends, I can promise you that the momentary satisfaction of that thing you thought would fulfill you will leave you empty—emptier than you can imagine. God and His love are truly the only things that can give us the sustaining satisfaction for our aching souls. Know that He is ready to meet you where you are right now and every following day. The Lord rewards those who seek Him, and a daily dose of seeking brings many rewards we can't even fathom.

Dependence is "the state or quality of being dependent, especially the quality or state of being influenced or determined by or subject to another." Let's switch over to being more and more influenced by God and His will. This state of dependence also imparts consistency. If we practise disciplined dependence on God, He can and will grant us more of His grace, mercy, and love. Simply put, we will have access to him in a deeper way, in a more trusting way, and in a more fulfilling way. And when we have that, we can and will live more victoriously.

Recently I found myself talking like a broken record to my kids. My twin boys seem to go through our house in a whirlwind, leaving what I call a "path of destruction" behind them. It seems everywhere I go I see signs of them and what they were just doing: wet towels, socks, leftover lunch from school, backpacks, shoes, hoodies—you name it! Everything is on the floor, and it leads to them. So, I found myself saying, as I feel I have hundreds of times, "Guys, when you come in, put your stuff away! Pick up after yourself ... *yada* ... I keep picking up after you and the messes you leave, and it's exhausting." I was thinking that their day and mine would go so much smoother if they did these few simple things on a regular basis. Why couldn't they get this? And then it hit me: God is saying the same kind of things to us! "Child, you are going through your day in a whirlwind and leaving a path of destruction. There is an easier way." Can you relate? I know you can—I know you can! How many of us start our days in chaos, spew words to people that nobody needs to hear, and end our days frustrated and with no peace? There is a better way. Let's depend on God for all of it. Would you be willing to try with me? I am still on the learning curve, and we would be doing it together. This book contains what I have learned so far, but I am still walking it out. I am still learning to calm the winds and find the peace, to add prayer to my coffee, and to talk to God all day long as if He is sitting right next to me in jeans and a T-shirt.

There are many things we can depend on God for. The list could be endless, and our own personal lists are near and dear to our hearts. Matthew 7:7–8 says, *"Ask, and it will be given to you; seek, and you will find; knock, and it will be opened to you. For everyone who asks receives, and he who seeks finds, and to him who knocks it will be opened."* From this we can learn to give up the control we think we have over our lives. When we ask God to lead us, to guide us, and to direct our steps, and when we agree with the Creator of the universe, we have access to freedom and peace. Want a free way to live? Depend on God to walk you on the path *He* chooses. It may not be the path you would have chosen, but it is where the blessings are! I don't know about you, but that is exactly where I want to be—where the blessings are. James 1:25 says, *"He who looks into the perfect law of liberty and continues in it and is not a forgetful hearer but a doer of the work, this one will be blessed in what he does."*

There are a few key items that we are going to be focusing on as we delve into dependence. The people in the referenced scriptures knew the exact same things! If you think about it, there is a reason they went to Jesus, and it was simply because they knew they could; they counted on Him in a huge way. *His name carried with it a certainty and a truth that people near and far sought after.* When it comes to depending on God, there is so much we can go to Him for. Even as you read this, your mind is probably racing with things you may want to ask for but haven't, or perhaps you have a list of things you already know, and you're ready to go. We are going to grow this list so that you can depend on Him in new ways and grow your relationship with Him. Yes, it's kind of like homework right now! When I started my walk, I had no idea I could go to God with a question any time of day and ask for an answer. Really—I was so new to the idea of constant connection, yet I wanted it more than anything! I didn't understand the whole conversation concept. I knew He had saved me, and He loved me, but I had no idea how amazingly personal our relationship could and would be. So, we are going to explore the realm of ideas that we can go to Him for. It may seem trivial, but it's important. For me it's been a huge learning curve as I have talked with other Christians about how God is woven into their days. I've learned from them, and I hope you can benefit from my experiences. Ultimately, this is God tapping you on the shoulder, saying, "C'mon, let's go."

First I would simply like to start with the fact that we *can* depend on God. This is where some people stop—or never get started. I mean, it's one thing to believe in Him and be saved, and it's quite another to surrender all things, every day, to Him. Most people are somewhere in the middle. It's understandable that you depend on God to help you with a sick or rebellious child, but perhaps you will deal with the finances on your own. Let us just start where we are and go from there. Let's take what we already give Him and choose one more thing tomorrow. After all, friend, He wants it all; He wants to *help* you with it all.

Let me sidestep a moment. I do believe that there is a lie the enemy would love to have you believe—the lie that you can't trust God, the lie that He really doesn't care or can't give you the desires of your heart. Dear one, don't believe this lie. Be courageous enough to have faith that you really can depend on our beautiful Savior. He is at the door of your heart, waiting to be let in.

Okay, so before we dig into what we can depend on him for, let's continue to explore the idea that we *can* run to our God; we *can* lay ourselves at His feet. Hesitation aside, friend, just go with me here; it will be worth it. Let's discover the truth that we *can* bring him our baggage, our fears, our joys, etc. We *can* depend on Him! All the people referenced in the beginning of this book knew they could. So *we* can too. 1 John 4:15–16 says, *"If anyone acknowledges that Jesus is the Son of God, God lives in them and they in God. And so, we know and rely on the love God has for us."* The reason we can depend on Him is that we can trust Him to be Himself!

We are going to explore some of the names of God, so we can firmly establish *who* He is before we move on. Here's why. Human nature is such that we go to those who we know or whose role we understand. For example, if we want a horseshoe fixed, we don't go to the grocery store; we go to the blacksmith. If we need an oil change, we don't go to the hairdresser; we go to the mechanic. If we need to buy fresh fruit, we don't go to the dry cleaners; we go to the local farmer. There are people of whom we *know* their purpose, their job, their identity to us. The farmer and the mechanic and the blacksmith have other identities to other people, because they are fathers and sons and friends and so on. But they have a specific identity to each of us. We need to radically enlarge the list of ways we identify God, identify with God, or identify Him from his Word. When we do this, we can go to him for *more* things, because we now understand that we can—because of *who He is*. Are you with me so far?

Too many of us have a limited scope to view God and His roles in our lives. Yes, I said role(s)—plural. This includes me, in a huge way. It goes without saying that we grow into most of it. Sometimes, though, it is as simple as being made aware. Many of us need to open our minds and hearts to the idea that God can satisfy multiple purposes to us. I don't think it's an accident that He referred to himself with a plethora of names. He wants us to know Him in all the ways that can and will make us whole. For example, I identified with Jesus immediately, His saving blood my new lifeline. Little did I know how much I would sharpen my discernment through the Holy Spirit or how much I would take comfort in God as Father, considering I grew up fatherless. We have needs He wants to fill and broken hearts He wants to mend. We need to let Him in on the good, the bad, and especially the ugly stuff. For now, let's continue to explore the names of God, so we may hopefully see Him in a new light.

CHAPTER 2

What's in a Name?

ASSESSING THE NAMES OF GOD IS A VERY PRACTICAL thing to do. I can tell you after studying it a bit that it is also an incredible thing to do. Looking at and learning the names of God allows us to understand the depth of His character, which in turn gives us the diverse options of how and why to count on Him. Remember, we are talking about depending on God here. The more ways we know Him, the more we can relate, depend on, and ultimately glorify Him. 1 Corinthians 10:31 tells us, *"Therefore, whether you eat or drink, or whatever you do, do all to the glory of God."*

Throughout Old Testament Scripture, God reveals Himself through different names to show us His character. Names in Old Testament times were more than a way to identify; they often had special meanings. As we look at all the different ways God chose to identify and characterize Himself, we can see that some of them demand respect and honour, and some show us how intimate His love is for us; it's quite amazing. I am constantly in awe at His love, His communion with us, and His desire to have us close to Him. The reality is that there is not one name that can fully convey the fullness of all He is and does. He reveals Himself with many names on purpose, and it's the collective list that shows us a glimmer of His majesty.

Psalm 148:13 advises, *"Let them praise the name of the Lord, for His name alone is exalted; His glory is above the earth and heaven."* So then, let's start there. Remember, this is a short list, not inclusive of all the names of God used in the Bible. Perhaps a side note here should add that I am not an expert in this. This is my homework for us. It is worth your while to do it too. There are books on this topic and tons of material. The subject is rather fascinating, but for my purposes here, I have simply done a quick synopsis.

Yaweh

The most commonly used name for God in the Old Testament (more than six thousand times) is *Yaweh*; it means "Lord" and "Jehovah." The vowels were added in current times; it was formerly just YWH and was not even to be spoken, because the name held such great power. This name denotes "omnipotence" and "ruler." It is built on the word for "I am." Yaweh is most famously known from God's interaction with Moses (Exodus 3), where He referred to Himself as "I Am." The name Yaweh not only confirms his existence but, more importantly, His presence. When it comes to depending on Him, it's amazingly wonderful to me to know that no matter where I am or what I am doing, He is present! How many of us depend on people who are not present, either physically or, worse yet, emotionally? Sometimes the people we need the most are caught up in their own fights and turmoil and are not available to us or for us. God, however, is present always.

Okay, you may know this, but I didn't, so just in case, I'll describe how some of the names work. There is a descriptive prefix and then a modifier indicating a quality, for example, Jehovah Jireh. In this example, *Jehovah* means "the Lord" and *Jireh* means "will provide" so that the name means "The Lord will provide." Now let's explore the names of *El*.

Elohim (Genesis 1:1)

The next most commonly used name for God in the Old Testament (more than two thousand times) is *Elohim*, which means "God," "Judge," "Creator." This name allows us to see God as the beginning, in the beginning, and judging over the universe He created. What comforts me in this name is knowing that I have a righteous and merciful Judge to look over my life, actions, and heart. I don't have to worry about what people think about me. I could choose to worry about this, but because I am grounded in God, I won't (most of the time.) Far too many of us let the world judge us; yet there is only One true Judge. We can easily be set free from so much anxiety and grief if we would only let our perfect Judge be the *only* judge in our personal worlds.

El Olam (Genesis 21:22–34)

Also used is *Elolam*, which means "Everlasting God." Isn't it amazing to know that our wonderful God never changes? We serve an unchanging God! The way He was is the way He will always be. So the truth and love that embody Him are always there for us to access. I saw a church sign during the month of January on which was written, "New year, new hope, same God." How fitting! In the New Testament, Jesus referred to Himself as the alpha and omega (Revelation 22:13), God from the beginning to the end and everything in between. That's where we are, in the middle, being carried along by His grace. His desire to reconcile His people to Himself never changes. He will always pursue the hearts that have gone astray. What a beautiful love story. By the way, it's *our* story.

It's not meant for someone else, but for you and me, every day of our lives.

El Shaddai

El Shaddai means "Lord God Almighty." This is the name that defines God as all-sufficient. There is nothing lacking in the God that we serve. When we need Him, He has all the answers, all the provisions, and all the tender love, mercy, and truth we could ever need. Remember, He stretched out His hands and created the stars. His resources are unending, along with His divine ways to soothe our weary souls. Doesn't it make sense that we would go to the One whose resources are unending when we need something? When I am praying through something, God never says to me, "Sorry, Tammy, I gotta go; I'm really busy right now. Can we talk a bit more later?" I mean, really! It could be hours and hours and days. His ear is always open; his Big Daddy lap always has room for me. People, on the other hand, don't have unlimited resources. My daughter moved away to school this year, and we usually talked every day on the phone. I was always, *always* glad to hear from her. But I must tell you, and she will attest to the truth of this, I was often making dinner, driving, grocery shopping, or working, and I would say, "Sweetie, I love you, but I have to go." God never has to go.

El Elyon (Genesis 14)

Along with Yaweh and Elohim, this name furthers the ultimate power and rulership names of God. This particular name means "The Most High God" and conveys God's supremacy. The idea of supreme is "the best of the best of the best." Yet we have no clue what that even means. God's supremacy is more than we can fathom. His perfect love, His perfect truth, His perfect will, His perfect ways, and His perfect thoughts are all wrapped up into

Creator, Ruler, Saviour—wow! There is no lie, nothing imperfect about Him. I don't know about you, but when you really have a problem, like a really I-gotta-talk-to-someone-and-work-through-this-or-I-am-going-to-go-crazy kind of problem, who would you rather talk to—the imperfect, never-really-going-to-know-every-single-thing-you-really-need-to-know person in your life (no matter how wonderful) or the Supreme one-and-only God? Let's face it: people, no matter how wonderful, are imperfect. They are tainted with judgement, negative experiences, and emotions; we all are. We cannot expect people to be what we really, really, really deserve: perfection. Yes, we deserve the perfection of God. He made us for it. He made us for Him. It just makes sense that we depend on Him.

El Roi (Genesis 16)

The last of the *El* names of might and power I will discuss is *El Roi*, which is the "God of Seeing." This name was ascribed to God by Hagar who, in her distress, fled to the wilderness. (Can anyone relate?) Did you ever want to run away and hide when things got really hectic? That's what Hagar did. Alone and desperate, she was then visited by an angel from God, sent to give her comfort and mercy. In her worst moment, God saw her and was there to comfort her. It's no different for us. While some of us suffer in silence, our God sees, knows our pain, and desires to bring us comfort. Psalm 121 substantiates this:

> *I will lift up my eyes up to the hills—*
> *From whence comes my help?*
> *My help comes from the Lord, Who made heaven and earth.*
> *He will not allow your foot to be moved; He who watches over you will not slumber.*
> *Behold, He who keeps Israel shall neither slumber nor sleep.*

> The Lord is your keeper; the Lord is your shade at your right hand.
> The sun shall not strike you by day, nor the moon by night.
> The Lord shall preserve you from all evil; He shall preserve your soul.
> The Lord shall preserve your going out and your coming in
> From this time forth, and even forevermore.

I am particularly comforted by the fact that God sees all. There are moments when this truth is my private and quiet shame, but for the most part I take extreme comfort in knowing that He knows everything. This means I can count on Him to know the tiniest details of my heart, my thoughts, my aches and desires, and the way my heart beats for Him. How did he know David had a heart like His? Because He sees all. Here it is again from the New Testament, Matthew 6:18. *"So that it will not be obvious to others that you are fasting, but only to your Father, who is unseen; and your Father, who sees what is done in secret, will reward you."*

Good so far? Okay, let's move on to the names preceded by Jehovah. (Remember, this prefix means "the Lord.")

Jehovah Raah (Psalm 23)

"The Lord my Shepherd." This specific name helps us see the intimate, human side of God, who takes our hands and leads us. When I think of life, day-to-day life, I know that I don't have it all figured out. I don't have all the answers. I giggle as I write this, because—let's be real—some days I have *no* answers! What I want is a guide. God, our "shepherd," is more than that. Shepherds care deeply about their flock and go seeking any one that goes astray. So does our God (Matthew 18:11–14). I do not need a guide who sends me off in a direction yet doesn't care whether I get there or not or how the journey goes. A Saviour who will shepherd me? Yes, that is exactly what I need! How about you? Doesn't this sound a lot more like what we could use every day?

Jehovah Rapha (Exodus 15:26)

"The Lord Who Heals." God is the healer of our bodies, minds, and souls. He uses miracles and He uses medicine. He can cure sickness in our bodies and minds, seen and unseen. He can (and let me say *desires* to) heal our hearts. His healing means our restoration. What is hurting, broken, or sick in you? You may not have ever thought to ask Him for healing, but you can. I have learned that sometimes He takes my headache away and sometimes He doesn't. I know, it's a simple example, but from a headache all the way to cancer and everything in between, we can ask! He is the One who knows the timing and necessity of our healing, but He is the ultimate physician. I mean, after all, He made us and knows us. Try laying down the sickness or brokenness at His feet and giving it to Him. I am not trying to make light of this topic; on the contrary, I encourage you to go to Him in this manner.

He gave us Jesus, the restorer of our souls. That, my friends, is the ultimate healing. He bridged the gap from earth to heaven, so we can be with Him in heaven. Yet He, in all His love and mercy, is willing to bind up and heal the deepest wounds we have, if we would just ask Him and walk it out with Him. Easy? Not always. Well, not usually. But vigilance is key in knowing and believing that healing can and will be ours after tragedy and wounding. It is so, so worth the fight. Remember, it only takes a mustard seed of faith put in Him, not efforts or works. When it comes to choosing who or what I want to depend on, I want to count on the One who I know desires my wholeness more than anything.

Jehovah Jireh (Genesis 22:13–14)

"The Lord Who Provides." The Lord will see to it that provision is there. When, you ask? He has our provisions in the palm of His hand. We need to know and ask in faith. When Abraham was willing to sacrifice Isaac, God provided a ram in the thicket. His provision was waiting, and sometimes ours is too. Do the eyes of our hearts see what He has provided, or are we looking elsewhere? Expect His favour. Thank Him for it. When it comes to understanding the *Lord Who Provides*, the experience in knowing this truth comes from laying our need down at His feet and thanking Him for the provision before it comes. That's faith, and that's what He wants to see from us. People in our lives may have good intentions but won't always know what is best for us, so choose to depend on our Jehovah Jireh to provide what is truly good and right for all circumstances.

Jehovah Tsidkenu (Jeremiah 23:6)

"The Lord our Righteousness." God's actions are always good, always pure, and always the truth. Everything He does is done with righteousness. He alone is the source of all righteousness, all things that are right and good in Him. When it comes to the aspect of depending on God, it seems clear that we humans can only strive for righteousness. There is not one person we can look to who can give us that, nor can we give it. Yet what we do have is access to a God, who loves us and directs us in righteous judgement and purpose. He is worthy of our love, attention, and surrender.

Jehovah Shalom (Judges 6:24)

"The Lord is Peace." I don't know about you, but when I look around, I don't see too many people with true peace. I do hear very often,

"When I do such and such, then I will be peaceful" or "If I could just do/have —— I would feel so much peace." The enemy has a lot of people chasing things: jobs, spouses, bank account balances, et cetera, for peace. We have access to a gracious God, who *is* peace. He covers us with peace, and He infuses us with His peace. Philippians 4:7 says it like this: *"Peace of God, which transcends all understanding, will guard your hearts and your minds in Christ Jesus."* Not only do we have access to it 24/7, but it is a guard. If we look at it from the opposite angle, from lack of peace, anxiety is what we may see. Being anxious is a huge tool of the enemy. We may become anxious over the future or the past, but truth be known, these do not even exist. Peace is accessed moment by moment, as we surrender to God and let Him directly rule and cover our steps—rule with His grace, direct with His purpose, and cover with His peace.

Jehovah Shammah (Ezekiel 48:35)

This name translates to "The Existing One." Literally, this means, "The Lord is there." Really, God is here, there, and everywhere. It's not that He was or will be but that he *is*. His existence has no boundaries, no limits. It's good news for us that He is right here, right now, in every aspect of our lives. He is here, but it's just that we don't let Him into our circumstances or acknowledge this truth. When we serve God continually, He reveals Himself to us. No masks. No hiding. No secrets. Unfortunately, people are rarely like that. Why not depend on a God who exists in truth, in all things, exactly the way you need Him to?

Abba

This section on the names of God is by no means complete or exhaustive. In fact, I think it is just the tip of the iceberg. From Elohim, the first name used in the Old Testament, to Abba, the last one given in the New Testament, God has been given hundreds of names. *Abba* translated means "like a child would address his father" or "Daddy." This name is not meant to diminish or undermine His authority and awesomeness (Psalm 47:2); rather, it symbolizes the kind of relationship He wants with us. The love of the Father is tender, gentle, merciful, and kind, to say the least. His heart cares deeply and His care for us is that of a good, loving father.

Perhaps I am naïve. Perhaps I have been granted an amazing kind of faith. I grew up without a father. Father figures did not do well by me either. I craved love and affection my whole life, and when I learned God could be a good father, I simply said "okay". There was no fight, no fuss—just acceptance. His faithfulness as my Father could fill the rest of the pages in this book.

Jesus

The learning continues as I move on to Jesus, who also has many names. The "Son of the Father," who is our redeemer, has upwards of fifty names in the Bible. Most of us know the most prominent and repeated ones: Prince of Peace (Isaiah 9:6), King of Kings (Revelation 17:14), Lord (Philippians 2:9–11), Lamb of God (John 1:29), Messiah (John 1:41), Good Shepherd (John 10:11), and Light of the World (John 8:12).

I have just a few more that are beautiful and continue to exemplify the mercy, kindness, and love of God. Here are just a few that I think are magnificent, just like Him.

Advocate: 1John 2:1. *My little children, these things I write this to you so that you do not sin. And if anybody does sin, we have an Advocate with the Father—Jesus Christ, the righteous.*

Mediator: 1Timothy 2:5. *For there is one God and one Mediator between God and men, the Man Christ Jesus.*

Rock: 1 Corinthians 10:4. *For they drank of that spiritual Rock that followed them, and the Rock was Christ.*

The Door: John 10:9. *"I am the door. If anyone enters by Me, he will be saved, and will go in and out and find pasture."*

The Way: John 14:6. *Jesus said to him, "I am the way, the truth, and the life. No one comes to the Father except through Me."*

The Word: John 1:1. *In the beginning was the Word, and the Word was with God, and the Word was God.*

True Vine: John 15:1. *"I am the true vine, and My Father is the vinedresser."*

There is so much to learn about the names of God that whole books have been written on the topic. There are literally hundreds of names listed in Scripture. I am simply highlighting some of them to affirm the beautiful and complete nature of our God. From the few examples above, we see the summary of His character that we can count on: He is ever-present, will provide, will heal our bodies and souls, will see our circumstances and our hearts; He is, was, and will always be. For some of us this list could bring up anger, frustration, or confusion. I know this, because it is the human condition and the mystery of God all wrapped into one. It brings up questions like Where? Why then? and How? We may ask, "If God is ever-present, where was He when …?" or "If He loves me so much, then why did I have to go through that?" We may have additional tough questions that relate to us individually and specifically, and the journey through this book may have some of the answers we are looking for. When we want to go deeper (where the answers are), we are usually called to do some digging. We can't find buried treasure without putting shovels in the ground! We must embrace the opportunity that God gives us to find Him. He is delighted when we search for him.

CHAPTER 3

The Faith Story

A MAJOR BENEFIT OF KNOWING THAT WE CAN DEPEND on God is that it helps us understand our faith. Faith is a huge topic. In secular circles and certainly around the water cooler, it is not the topic most people wish to speak of. Faith, like religion, is considered a bit personal, to say the least, for most common conversations. The two things, faith and religion, are not the same. Religion I wont touch; faith I do wish to talk about. Faith is spoken about as a gift of the Spirit (Romans 12:3); it is part of the armour of God (Ephesians 6:16), and it is 100 per cent connected to living victoriously.

Ephesians 2:8–9 says, *"For by grace you have been saved through faith, and that not of yourselves; it is the gift of God, not works, lest anyone should boast."* The first and foremost thing our faith does is allow us to receive salvation, to be saved. I am sure that you are aware of the biblical benchmark and meaning of faith. Hebrews 11:1 tells us, *"Now faith is the substance of things hoped for, the evidence of things not seen."* This faith is in something we cannot see; it is in God, whose Son died for us not in our time but a long time prior. His Spirit is with us, though we cannot see it with our human eyes. We understand faith, as we have been saved. Yet the knowledge of what to do with our faith in our daily lives can sometimes elude us.

The faith story immediately follows the names of God for a reason. It is when we know who God is and what He is about—and only then—that we can understand what to do with our faith. I will tell you that this had my mind messed up for a while. You see, it's not about how much faith we have but rather what we do with it. Does our faith grow? Absolutely. Can we increase it? Of course. It's just that right now you already have enough. Remember how God described some faith that works? Luke 17:6: *"So the Lord said, 'If you have faith as a mustard seed, you can say to this mulberry tree, "Be pulled up by the roots and be planted in the sea," and it would obey you.'"* You see, we don't need much. We just need to take our faith and put it into action. Okay, stay with me here. He, Himself, is the object of our faith. When (not if) He asks us to follow Him and to do something, it is usually way out of our comfort zones. Perhaps I am talking just to myself here, but I wanted *more* faith before. I really thought I needed more faith to accomplish His task, dream, or purpose in my life. I used to think, *If I had more faith, I could surrender more quickly, be more obedient, follow more easily, hear better, and walk it out faster.* And then I would ask myself, *"What is wrong with me? "* It was not until recently that I reread this passage from Luke and saw it differently. Because I know *who* He is and have faith in Him alone, I learned that I don't need more. What I have is just enough. Guess what? The same is true for you!

I can tell you from my own experience that when I accepted my situation, the good with the bad, and put my faith in God, He was able to do His mighty work. I would that bet many others have similar stories. We need to take the faith we have in Him and put that faith in His ability to do what He does. The problem is that most of the time we are in the way and telling ourselves of our faith. Yes, we do have faith. But it must be placed where God can use it—in Him and His character. Carrying our faith like a blanket all wrapped up isn't going to do us any good. We need to unfold it and place it over the situation that needs it. This is bringing action to our faith. Shake out your blanket, and let God do His thing. *Having* faith isn't enough. We need to *place* it where it belongs: on God and His abilities. This whole section was written so we could know, without the shadow of a doubt, that God is able and willing, without limits, to do mighty and wonderful things. His character is all truth, love, and might; therefore, His actions are that way as well.

God must be the object of our faith. This current road He has taken me on—which includes roles of wife, mother, friend, writer, encourager, woman of faith—I can manage! Because He Who is the Everlasting God, the All-Sufficient One, The All-Seeing One, The Provider, and the Healer, has asked me and lives in me. Thus I now place my faith in Him to do those things in me.

I understood faith before, but there seemed to be pieces missing. Those gaps kept me from having as much victory as I ought. It is crucial that we continue to desperately ask questions, to seek answers and wisdom from Him. We must stay open, because He is faithful and does answer. It is amazing how and when those "aha" moments come. God is for us. He wants to see us victorious. Matthew 7:7–8 says, *"Ask, and it will be given to you; seek, and you will find; knock and it will be opened to you. For everyone who asks receives, and he who seeks finds, and to him who knocks it will be opened."* So count on God, depend on God, and believe Him when He says He will help. Instead of asking Him last, ask Him first. Don't go to all the wrong people when you need help. Go to Him, who knows all the details already. Just get to the point, cut to the chase, and invite Him into every detail.

When it comes to our faith, increasing the amount we have is a natural transition, but know it is not necessary for victorious living, as just discussed. We go from asking to claiming, from wondering to thanking. *Asking is belief, claiming is faith*! When we depend on Him and He acts in amazing ways in our lives, we have more to stand on, and our faith grows. The thought that our faith is insufficient or powerless, is a lie. When we understand that a mustard seed is enough, and when we truly understand what to do with even miniscule amounts of faith, we become very dangerous in the Kingdom. We become dangerous to the enemy, because we see him for what he is, a liar and a stealer of joy. We learn to recognize his schemes. We become weapons of the spiritual war that wages around us for the kingdom of God, and we draw a line in the sand that says, "the lies stop here and now." The enemy wants us to believe that the faith we have is unusable—don't believe it! God is bigger than any problem. Beware of thoughts that God can solve other people's problems but not yours! This, of course, is not true at all. He has the way, the idea, and the solution. When we have faith, we can say, "I believe you, Lord. I'm all in, and I am counting on you."

This past winter I had to travel to a city I had not been to before, and I had to use my GPS to get there. The trek took me on the highway, and not so long onto my trip I found myself behind a transport truck. Because of the time of day, the highway was very, very busy, and I found that I was kind of stuck there. Getting stuck behind a large truck is frustrating; it is difficult because you cannot see the road or anything ahead. Were it not for the little black box telling you "Turn right here!" you'd miss the exits, and who knows where you'd end up. This was in the winter, and right about this time it started to snow quite heavily. Not only could I not see the path before me due to the truck, I got really distracted with wipers and just trying to see out my window at all. I was tempted to get off the highway and stop somewhere so I could figure out a better way to get there. Eventually I decided this was the best route to take, and I saw an exit. As I put on my indicator light to make the right turn, so did the transport in front of me! *"What? Are you kidding me? This cannot be happening!"* Off went the blinker, and I stayed on the highway. I thought I could get away from the blockage in front of me, go around it or something. But despite my efforts, it was still going to be there. I made a quick and right decision to follow faithfully the instructions given to me by the GPS, and eventually I got to where I needed to be. The trip took much longer with the busy road, poor visibility, and snow, but I got there!

When it comes to faith, let's look at it like this. God has given each of us a task, dream, or journey. He has given us an endpoint. He is the GPS. The roads we must follow may not be visible at times; the way might be unclear, and life's storms might come along and distract us. But our faith, whatever the amount, is enough for us to place it in Him, so He can guide us, even through storms, onto the right roads and to our predestined endpoints (Proverbs 3:5–6). He will get us to where He wants us to be. He wants to, and will, complete the work he has started in us (Philippians 1:6). We often think we know better and decide to abandon the instructions and figure it out ourselves. All this does is waste time. God is so wonderfully faithful, though, that He is willing to love us and teach us through this as well.

But You Said

There is a very wonderful phenomenon that happens to us when we learn to stand on what we know about God. When we immerse ourselves in the Word, when we pray and listen, when we see the goodness of God in our lives and know and hear His promises, we learn to say, "But You said." This simple quote puts God to work. Let me explain. I think it is safe to say that we often dig into faith when there is a problem or when we are believing for something. Once we have understood His Word and His promises, we can say them out loud: "Lord, I am struggling with —— today, but You said I am more than a conqueror, and I believe you. Thank you." Or it might be, "Lord, I am struggling with how I see myself today, but You said I am the apple of Your eye, your masterpiece, and Your prized possession. I believe You. Thank you." These are simple examples, yes, but you get the idea. A while ago I was heartsick over an illness my daughter had. God promised me that He would heal her. I cannot count how many days I paced my home, saying, "Lord, it doesn't look good today, but You said You would heal her, and I believe You. You said. You said. You said!" Take a promise, and let God know that you believe Him. Say it. Stand on it. Claim it.

This is the God we put our faith in, *"That He would grant you, according to the riches of His glory, to be strengthened with might through His Spirit in the inner man, that Christ may dwell in your hearts through faith; that you, being rooted and grounded in love, may be able to comprehend with all the saints what is the width and length and depth and height—to know the love Christ which passes knowledge; that you may be filled with all the fullness of God* (Ephesians 3:16–19). We put our faith in a God whose love and might are incomprehensible. He loves us more than enough to let us jump right into believing and claiming that He is all He says He is.

Sweet Surrender

Depending on God requires a step first that may make some of us uncomfortable—*surrender*. For many people the word surrender has a negative connotation, but it's just how you look at it. For many of us, when we were growing up surrender was something you did with the candy you were eating right before dinner or the water balloons you'd made while nobody was looking and were about to launch out of your bedroom window. While surrender does impart a giving up of something, what we are referring to here is a giving up of something that is harming us or simply a relenting to another's will. Since God's will is perfect, and because it is pure and out of perfect love, His will cannot hurt us.

Here's the thing. Surrender, in and of itself, leads us to depending on God, to digging in to Him and literally clinging on for dear life. When we let go and say, "Yes, Lord," the very next steps are to ask His direction, get instruction, seek wisdom and discernment, stand on what we know, and take steps of faith. I now see the word *surrender* as so much more and so beautiful; I can *feel* it, soft and wonderful, like a big hug. Surrender is like a bridge supported by the weight of obedience that brings us closer to Him. When I first started feeling God asking me to surrender parts of myself, I wasn't sure how it would work or what it meant. I had grown up with ginormous walls around my heart, and so this was a whole new kind of life for me. According to *Merriam-Webster's* dictionary, surrender is "to agree to stop fighting, hiding, resisting," etc. (because you know that you will not win or succeed) or what I think applies here even more: "to give the control or use of something to someone else." Thus, to surrender to God is to give up control of our daily lives to Him.

If we could learn to surrender every moment as it unfolded, can you imagine the peace we could experience or the joy we could uncover? In this surrender, then, what exactly are we surrendering to? We are yielding to the beautiful presence of God, to His grace, to His glory, and *for* His glory. Lastly, of course, we are giving in to His beautiful and perfect will for us. We are told to *"love the Lord God with all your heart, with all your soul, with all your mind, and with all your strength"* (Mark 12:30). That's a tall order to fill. There is only so much room in a human heart, only so much understanding in a human brain, and not enough awareness of our human soul and what it needs. Without surrender we cannot even begin to fulfil this obligation. We must relinquish parts of ourselves and allow God to fill them with Himself. *There is no other way.*

Again, let us learn to know and rely on the God who loves us. Every new name we adopt for Him is an opportunity for us to connect with Him in a deeper way. These new connections widen our hearts. If we think about it, it's very simple. We must learn to know God in more ways and grow our relationships to new heights and depths. We must open ourselves up to more of His love and more of His mercy. We can gain experience and stand on what we know. We need to *know* and *rely*. It is probable at that point that He will ask us to do some crazy thing we never thought possible, like write a book or something! You know what I mean. As we come to know Him more, we learn to rely on Him more. Then we learn to place our faith in Him more, but because faith is an action word, it usually means walking something out (or sometimes just getting out of the way)—like this book, your marriage, a mission, etc. We *must* continually seek truth, take His hand, and walk things out. That is the faith journey, and that is why we depend on Him.

God is readily available to those who call on Him and those who wish to know Him more. He is like a diamond that you hold up to the light and see in a plethora of angles. As soon as you turn the jewel a little, the light changes, and the view is different again. Throughout this book we will turn The Jewel, to see Him in a different way, so we can go deeper still, learn more, live a bit differently, appreciate more, and find more joy—in Him.

Depending on God allows us to have more freedom and more victory. I have been able to (re)discover Him and experience a higher level of joy and freedom for sure—and I absolutely needed it! I had accumulated (perhaps you can identify) a lot of baggage in the thirty years before I met our gracious Saviour, and I had my share of new stuff as He worked to free me from the strongholds of my past. He came to set the captives free; I had most definitely been captive! When we share our hearts with Him, our lives become less complicated and more focused on the goal of knowing Him, especially knowing His will for each of us.

My heart aches to know God. I yearn to experience Him as much as I can to create not just moments of peace and joy but a lifelong relationship with Him in which that peace and joy is a daily realization. My deepest desire is to pursue his will for me. This desire has been my greatest joy and at times my greatest challenge. My purpose is to seek Him *and* find Him, to hear Him *and* listen, and to ultimately do whatever He calls me to do. This will take a concentrated effort, not only of my mind but of my heart.

When we set a focused, single-minded course toward God, our souls soar. How, amid the chaos that life can bring, can we find peace and joy and freedom? With daily victorious living as our prize and Jesus as our guide, we can have the joy and freedom that we so desire.

The idea for this book first came to me around 2002; the idea was born, and the basic five principles laid out. In 2013, it became a study that I had the honour of teaching at two local churches. That opportunity allowed me to further my research and writing and, most importantly, my passion for this information, and I dove into creating this book in 2015. Little did I know that in January of 2016 I would be in a car accident that would injure me in many ways. The biggest difficulty was the brain injury I suffered as a result of a severe concussion. This has affected every part of my day-to-day functioning. The book project was stalled, and my entire life went into slow motion. It has been quite a journey, and although I would not ask for it again, I would certainly not wish it away. God has brought me through an incredible time since then, starting with everything I knew being turned upside down. But finally I am here, putting the finishing touches on this book—His book. Now, more than ever, my life is surrendered to Him, and I am grateful for the layers He peeled back and for the infusion I received of Him. I can see that some of the richest information came this year while I struggled with seeking His will, surrendering, resting, and finding peace. Those were the biggie lessons this last year, and I can honestly say I am in such a different place than before, a deeper, richer place in Him. I hope that translates into a deeper, richer read for you!

All right then, let's look at this just a little bit more, for some more confirmation that we are expected to know and rely on God. There are a few more scriptures to seal it up.

Isaiah 50:10 says, *"Who among you fears the Lord? Who obeys the voice of His Servant? Who walks in darkness and has no light? Let him trust in the name of the Lord and rely upon his God."*

Exodus 14:12–14 says, *"Is this not the that word that we told you in Egypt, saying, 'Let us alone that we may serve the Egyptians?' For it would have been better for us to serve the Egyptians than that we should die in the wilderness. And Moses said to the people, 'Do not be afraid. Stand still, and see the salvation of the Lord, which He will accomplish for you today. For the Egyptians whom you see today, you shall see no more forever.. The Lord will fight for you, and you shall hold your peace..'"*

Bridge the Gap

Sometimes God calls us to give over something or someone because it can only be something or someone that is getting in our way. When we are committed to God, to live out surrendering and following Him, that commitment can fill gaps in other places in our lives. The commitment we have in Him allows His love to cover us and build a bridge where there was a gorge. If you aren't sure how committed you are to your job, your commitment to God steps in and allows you to continue. If you're not sure how committed you are to your relationship or marriage, surrender it and commit to doing God's will. That commitment allows us to remain where we ought to. I cannot describe how many situations I did not think I could stand, stay in, or deal with; yet His love through them all filled the gap. Where my unbelief held me back, His unfailing love and strength built bridges where there were none. It was my commitment to Him alone that allowed it all to happen. Once you taste the goodness of His love it is almost unbearable not to surrender to it. Psalm 34:8 says, *"Taste and see that the Lord is good; Blessed is the man who trusts in Him!"*

When we want God and the relationship with Him more than anything, nothing is impossible. We can count on Him for more than we could ask for, think of, or believe. It starts with us wanting our souls to be watered, fed, and carried by the One who created us, the One who loves us and knows us better than anyone. We acknowledge that God is nudging us regarding something that we need to give over or stop fighting Him on, and then we work through the surrender. It is by obedience that we can do so, and the process ensures that we will go deeper. Know this: everything we give over is replaced by something better—something beautiful from Him!

God fills the gap with His love in His own way, and that love allows us to heal, to learn, and to grow. He will do this for us until we, in surrender and obedience to His purposes, get to the place He wants us. Let me qualify: this may not be easy. Following God's purpose, particularly if our wills are in opposition, can be very difficult. Truth be told, in that case it is impossible. Surrender is the key. It can be the most difficult thing you ever do. In fact, I will bet that obedience to God's plan will walk you into some of the most challenging circumstances of your life! Obedience is more than physically walking out what we know to be God's will. He demands more of us than that. He wants us to accept in our hearts first. The sin of disobedience is multi-layered. I believe disobedience is bred from several things, including unbelief, pride, and unforgiveness. Harbouring any of these can go undetected or ignored; we must be diligent to uncover and overcome any of them that God reveals within our hearts, no matter how much it hurts. Let's be frank—admitting any sin, especially those deeply ingrained in our psyche and daily living, is going to humble us. And chances are we have a lot of junk to work through. These things exist behind huge brick walls that need smashing down. It's good to know that this is God's specialty. Eventually, though (and from personal experience I can say it's true), the pain of being disconnected from God is more than we can bear, the distance from His love is more painful than the pain we have been avoiding, and we finally tell Him we are ready to move on. In His sovereignty, He may let our hearts break just enough to open us up to His way, His love, and His timing. Trust these three to be perfect for where you are and what you need. The truth is that the Maker of the universe knows *exactly* what you need!

Not Your Average Vitamin

Now the question is Who or what are we depending on? I'm not talking about the morning coffee or the vitamins we take for stamina. I'm talking about what or who, other than God, we are using as our crutches daily.

Does your closest girlfriend know every detail of your failing relationship, but God is only let in when you need a blessing in some other place in your life? Does your family know what financial struggles you have, but you haven't yet surrendered these to God? Is prayer something you do on Sundays only? Maybe the thought of allowing God to heal that disease is foreign to you. How much of your past or present hurts are you letting God in on? Let's get something clear right now: He knows anyway. He knows every detail of your coming and going, what is in your mind and heart. We established that earlier.

Why, then, do we pretend he doesn't know, or doesn't care, or can't help—or, worse yet, *won't* help? Friends, this is the challenge and the beauty of learning something new. Sometimes we get stuck on what we think about God. Some people put God in a box; they only know God in a certain way or ways, and beyond that His presence is foreign. Let's keep Him out of the box!

Regarding people, if we spend enough time with anyone, eventually they will let us down. People have faults. God, however, will not fail us. He is all truth and all love. Beyond our questions of Why? and How, then? we need to just *know* this within ourselves.

I was baptized at nineteen. I was full of fire and gratitude. I absolutely loved what Jesus was doing in my life and in my heart. I wanted everyone around me to know and to feel the same thing. But not everyone wanted to hear; not everyone wants to attack their past or their problems head-on or even at all. It wasn't long before I was alone in my new-found faith. The world around me soon stifled my fire, and I found myself facing the hardest time of my life. It was a short ten years. My roots were shallow, and I believed my shield of faith was unusable. When the storm came, it almost killed me. What happened next was the beginning of exactly what I am writing about now: dependence. I gave myself to Him so utterly and completely this time, and I allowed Him to penetrate every part of my being. This time I was thirty-one. A little more life had happened by now; I was married, with two children, college education, and so on. I was in a completely different season, and I approached it in a very different way. Everything I read, watched, and listened to was Word based, and I learned—but most important of all, I surrendered and depended! I depended day by day, because I knew the consequence of not doing so. I knew what could happen. Life brings storms; that's normal. So my point of reference changed. Depending on God every single day (okay, yes, hour by hour or minute by minute, in some circumstances) is like breathing. It's vital to life, vital to a healthy, victorious life; so I have learned. This is what I share. More importantly, this is *why* I share.

The truth of His character needs to permeate our marrow so that we can work through the questions and the days of our lives. Without this truth, we might not even see the need to try. And the enemy would love that, wouldn't he, seeing us stuck in our junk, not depending on God, not believing God, and being totally unfruitful? It's one or the other, the truth or the lie. Freedom or slavery; friends, choose freedom. Choose fruit. Choose to believe His truth. I cannot say that every season since then has been easy. I cannot say that every day of every year I have been a victor. No, that wouldn't be true. I have failed. I have lied. I have said the wrong thing too many times to count. I have been afraid. I have been angry and sad, and I have been ashamed, but (*sigh*) I lived through it all. My roots are deep now. I know who I am and to Whom I belong. I depend on my God as if the life is being squeezed out of my throat. That's what I am talking about. Grit. Dirt. Life. No sugar-coated God-is-good-and-you-will-never-see-the-real-me-because-i-am-wearing-a-mask kind of faith. What good is that? Yet it is the way a lot of us live. It's time to take off the masks and get down to the nitty-gritty real-life dependence that He so wants us to have. Isaiah 41:10 tells us, *"So do not fear, for I am with you; do not be dismayed, for I am your God. I will strengthen you and help you; I will uphold you with my righteous right hand."* I think that sums it all up.

Big or Small, He Wants It All

Right now, either in the margin (but not if you think you might pass this book along to a friend) or on a piece of paper—or hey, in your mind, if you're in a place where you can't write—list all the things that you depend on God for. Yes, really do it, and right now! And yes, breathing counts. For some of you this may take a while, but please do it, because there is a reason for it. I'd like you to think of this in two parts. The first is *What daily activities do you depend on God to get you through?* and the second is a more general question: *What do you depend on God for?* This would include the big stuff, like salvation and mercy.

It's important that we see how much we count on God for. Our lists may be healthy or may need improvement, but they provide a visual. They also make us aware of what needs to happen. We must acknowledge where we are at. If a list is rather short, then it indicates that dependence on Him is perhaps something that needs work. Remember that He delights in us counting on Him, and He wants to grow relationships with us from wherever we are *right now*.

Many people have never even really thought of it. Loving God and living devoted to Him may be natural, but thinking of a detailed list of what they depend or count on Him for has never crossed their minds. Perhaps through one of life's storms they've recognized that they felt a dependence for presence, healing, or peace, but then the storm passed. If we are not focused on living God-purposed, then we tend to go back to status quo. Hence the need for this activity. I have learned when I get into automatic-pilot mode or when I feel dry and thirsty for him to automatically ask myself this question: "How much am I depending on God in my day-to-day life?" The answer usually takes me off cruise control and back to purposely giving Him every detail, listening, praying, being in the Word, and walking out my faith instead of just talking about it. (Yes, we will most definitely be discussing this.) Friend, we have the same life—different details, different geography, different DNA, but the same life. The details of our lives differ, but broken is broken. Faith is faith. God is God. Heaven is later, and here is now. And as we have been discussing, *now* is the challenge.

Once you have done the list, hopefully it will be very clear what you can give over to Him so that He can rule that part of your daily activities. Here is a quick and simple example. My husband and I have twins, and when they were born I struggled with frustration a lot. We already had two girls, aged five and three, and the addition of twin baby boys wreaked havoc on me. I ran a business from home, and my husband also ran a very busy business, so we had our plates full. It wasn't too long before I was crying all the time. Hormones? Nope. It was my time—or lack thereof. Finally, I figured out that the details are what God wants, and I gave my schedule to God. Yes, I really did. This is a lesson I go back to and still reclaim. Every morning I would say, "Lord, I give it all to you today. You know how crazy my day can be. I have work appointments, groceries to get, meals to cook, laundry, doctor's appointments, and I'd love a shower. But, please, you already know where I need to be and when. Please get me there in your time; I am grateful that you have it all worked out for me. Thank you." I cannot express the dynamics of me and my home and how they changed for the better after I learned to give it over to Him. By the way, I still say that prayer, now more than ever. I need to, because those twins are now teenagers! This is a small example, and they only get better from there. Time and schedules are easy to give over … well, that's how it was for me. I learned that trying to control things was quite silly. It was another lie I saw for what it was—futile. Perhaps, though, the simple things like schedules are a great place to start. Can you imagine what He could do if we said, "Lord, here are my finances," or "Lord, here is my marriage," or "Lord, here are my children," or "Lord, I give you my job." Once we give Him something, we give Him more opportunity to work in our lives. That work creates relationship between us. That relationship draws us closer to Him, through prayer and listening, through growth in discernment and obedience. Every time we depend on God for something, it's like building a portfolio; there's just more and more we learn about Him. Hopefully, by the end of this chapter we will be strengthened and encouraged by seeing what we in fact depend on God for. We will have some fresh ideas on how to take it a bit deeper and rely on Him further.

What has rumbled in your spirit as something you can start depending on Him for? Perhaps you can take some time to see if He reveals something He would love to help you with. Use the margin or, better yet, a journal. It is a great idea to record the things (truths) God reveals to you, so you can look back at your journey. Remember what I said earlier: Stand on what you know. It's easier to do if you have recorded what He has impressed on your spirit.

Friend, let me be blunt. I am all for best friends, confidants, brotherly and sisterly love, and those people we just count on in our days. I love people—a lot. I am not in any way suggesting that we abandon the good people or relationships in our lives. What I *am* suggesting, however, is that God becomes the number-one go-to. I tell a few very close friends some circumstances of the tough stuff. We cry. We laugh. We pray. But you can bet I have already hashed it out with God or will be running to Him immediately afterward. I take advice in stride. I listen at arm's length, and I run it all through what I call a "God filter." It's great to talk and work through things with our favourite people, but ultimately I want to know what God wants me to do. Over the past couple of decades I have learned to lean into all the things just discussed. This chapter is not meant to steer you away from people, only to steer you closer to God. If

He wants you to steer clear of someone, He will tell you Himself. On the contrary, He may also put someone in your life to help you along. Paul had Silas and Timothy. David had Jonathan. God-given friends and helpers will appear. I have been a Jonathan, and I have had my share of godly women friends; I still do. But no one should replace our infinite and ever-merciful Lord and Saviour.

The Beautiful Struggle

I do not wish to count myself as one who is easily discouraged. I like to think of myself as a bit of a rebel warrior. In the past two years, life has really heaped it on—I mean really, really heaped it on. And when life heaps it on, we have to make choices. Instead of asking Why?, perhaps a more appropriate question could be How? ("Show me what to do" or "Show me what you require from me right now in this, Lord.") Deciding to look at hard times as opportunities to grow is a choice. It is also mandatory for victory. We must learn to pray for contentment in whatever season we are in and acquire the capacity to be content. In Philippians 4:11, Paul says, *"Not that I speak in regard to need, for I have learned in whatever state I am, to be content."* I believe wholeheartedly that this is something to strive for.

God knows what we need in *all* seasons, and it makes sense because, after all, He created us. He gave to us (as promises) all the things we would humanly ache for. God is, in fact, *more* than we can ever comprehend. He really can be the answer to our heart's desires ... if we would let Him. Since desire is the one human thing that is limitless, it is the one thing that can only be satisfied by the creator of the universe Himself, who also happens to be limitless. How fitting. How beautiful. How perfect. Herein lies the "beautiful struggle"—the surrendering of our very wills, longings, bare and unsatisfied, to Him who made us, so that He could fulfill the desires of our souls. (See Psalm 20:4, Psalm 21:2.) The giving up of the thing we want may not be the easiest thing to do, but it certainly is not the hardest. I believe that losing one's self to surrendering the ability to simply want or not, is the hardest. Let's be clear. Our love for God may prompt us to allow His grace to carry us through to the surrender of something. My question is, can it be enough to stop us from *wanting* at all? I believe that the core of the beautiful struggle is this: giving up just wanting, or not wanting; it's choosing to surrender the choice to surrender. Did you ever want something so much and all the while you knew it was wrong, yet you longed for it anyway? Sometimes we just want the right to want. Did you ever feel something so much that you just needed to *feel* it, even though it was the worst thing for you? That's it again. Grit. Dirt. Life. Surrender it. Struggle is resistance. Resistance is pain. This pain is so unnecessary.

If there is something or someone I want very much, I may hold onto the choice to simply want it. I may even understand that if I can get past this, God can carry me through the rest—but if I hold onto the ability to keep on wanting, I will be on very dangerous ground! We already know that desire is insatiable. Deluded hearts are dangerous, because the foundation of the desires is lies. When our desires move from being focused on Jesus to being focused on ourselves; when this happens, we get way off track. While we may not recognize when our hearts are deluded, we will absolutely notice that something has changed. That shift in focus from Jesus to self produces wants that are not heaven-based. They come with a self-justification of sin to attain the desire we wanted so strongly to have. God knows of this shortfall in our character. We must be open, be open, be open to the Spirit who convicts and teaches and be led by Him. I love these verses from Jeremiah that speak of exactly this: *"The heart is deceitful above all things, and desperately wicked: who can know it? I, the Lord, search the heart, I test the mind, even to give every man according to his ways, according to the fruit of his doings."* (Jeremiah 17:9–10)

Deluded hearts are so dangerous because they are a major ploy of the enemy. He seeks to derail us and keep us in so much inner turmoil that we get stuck. I have learned that getting caught up in the beautiful struggle unfolds this way; our deluded hearts want something that essentially is not part of God's plan, and therein lies the problem. The slippery slope of disobedience, self-justification, and sugar-coated rebellion sidetracks our purpose and sets us up for sin. When we are hungry enough for God, the slope can be short. We may find Him ripping the veils from our eyes and pouring the truth all over us.

Why have I said all this? Perhaps it seems off-track? This section, although very long, is still about *depending on God*. The point is that we know, without a doubt, that we need to be at His feet every day, however that may look to each of us. It may mean devotion in the wee hours of the morning before children are up, worship music in the car, talking to God as if He is sitting right there, or quietly closing our eyes and whispering to Him what is in our hearts. We need to stay connected, to keep the conversation open and fluid, so we can speak *and* hear. Depending on Him to know us, comfort us, and lead us is key.

Know that when we want something like wisdom, peace, or patience, for example, we are sometimes given the "opportunity to become" those things. God does not dish those things out on silver platters but rather allows us to grow in Him and with Him. Sometimes God wants to grow our perseverance through prayer and our faith through perseverance. He uses certain times and opportunities to stretch our faith, and the action is through prayer. Prayer is one of the best ways to know His will, to know the end point, so to speak, and to follow the GPS. Prayer is faith talk. It is required.

Paul put it this way: *"I say then; walk in the Spirit, and you shall not fulfill the lust of the flesh. For the flesh lusts against the Spirit, and the Spirit against the flesh; and these are contrary to one another, so that you do not do the things that you wish."* (Galatians 5:16–17) He understood the core of it. Don't be dismayed, though—he, too, struggled with walking it out. In his letter to the Romans he said this: *"There is none righteous, no not one."* (Romans 3:10) When describing his own journey, he says, *"For what I am doing, I do not understand. For what I will to do, that I do not practice; but what I hate, that I do."* (Romans 7:15) Can anyone relate?

Let's Talk About Truth

It's important to know that truth is multi-layered, which is how I like to think of it. There is God's truth, which is his Word, the living truth of the Bible. We need to know this Word, study this Word, and stand on it—it is *His Word*. Our lives are contingent on our dependence on it. When it comes to spiritual battle, there is no better weapon than the Sword of the Spirit, which is the Word of God. When it comes to speaking faith into our days and lives, there is no better way than through the Word of God. If He is all truth, then we need to know that truth. One of the most well-known scriptures is John 8:31–32, which says, *"Then Jesus said to those Jews who believed in Him, 'if you abide in My word, then you are my disciples indeed. And you shall know the truth, and the truth shall make you free.'"* What beautiful truth!

The second kind of truth is God's specific word over our lives. When the Maker of the universe shows you a path and a purpose, or an answer to a prayer, or any kind of personal truth at all, it's notably incredible. Hearing from Him always puts me in awe. There are different ways we hear from Him, and the messages vary from daily routine stuff to lifelong kinds of things—you know, big-picture versus little-picture stuff. We may get large visions regarding missions or ministry or smaller ones like the feeling we are to give someone a book or some groceries. All of this is super cool, because we are hearing from our God! It's proof that His fingertips are on our heads! But listen, friends; there is more.

This book is based on the ideal that we are to live whole and peaceful, God-centred lives; the reality is that we all have this thing called life going on. And it's hard sometimes. Sometimes? Yes, I know, that's an understatement! Many of us have lived through decades of hard times and pain, and some of us searched for "happy" or "normal" most of our lives. I was thirty-one when I recommitted my heart. Before that, I never knew deep-down happiness. You know what I mean—not the superficial happy, when you walk out a "typical" life, like college, marriage, kids, house, vacations, and Christmas trees. I mean that deep-down feeling of "I'm really okay." To be criticized, neglected, abandoned, and abused most of your life and then to live as an adult in a shut-down-the-heart-because-it's-easier state was like being part of the walking dead. Am I connecting to anyone here? To be without identity tore me apart. I am speaking candidly, because chances are someone will identify with me. I am sharing, with the prayer that you, too, need to hear this. We are going to talk more about identity in the next chapter, but here is the real-life application. There, I've planted the seed.

As we go broken to Him, He gently starts to heal us. Pay attention, because this is crucial! *Healing can only come when we replace our own truth with His.* His truth over our very own hurts and broken hearts, is all we will ever need. In the quietness of listening, prayer, and time with Him, we can ask those questions that haunt us; we can unburden the resentment, anger, or perhaps some unforgiveness that has taken root, and we can ask for His specific truth.

Perhaps you're in a marriage that's going through hard times. In your time with God, you ask Him to speak His truth to you, and you hear from Him this truth: "You *can* do it. This is where you belong, and I will be with you." Perhaps you've had a diagnosis of a debilitating medical condition. Your truth is that you're preparing for the worst. His truth may be that for His glory you will minister to those around you and He will sustain you.

It's as if God breathes new life into our dry bones with His beautiful truth. How many of us would gladly receive a new truth to help us persevere through something extremely difficult? I'm sure all of us would! Once we are tired of being victims, aware we have been believing and living with the enemy's lies, or tired of the unfruitfulness of our lives, we may be willing to do whatever it takes. That's when He speaks His truth. I said it before, but it is worth saying again. *Be so hungry for Him and His truth that the noise of life fades away.* We must look up, focus on Him, depend on Him, and then walk it out. Right, I've said that already too. I know what you're thinking, and no, there's not much more to it than this!

I heard it said and I believe the validity of the statement that people are motivated by one of two things (in the search for truth): inspiration or desperation. I first sought Him out of desperation. I had been so broken that I ached for Him to patch the cracks, fill the holes, and put me back together. Yes, it happened more than once. I have searched over and over for truth. I received a more wonderful and deeper healing when I asked for His truth over a specific situation. But here is what's cool: *"I can do all things through Christ who strengthens me."* (Philippians 4:13) This scripture has a new meaning for me now. My growth is not always from desperation now. There is a beautiful amount of inspiration from knowing His utter splendour splashed with desperate moments this life throws at me.

The truth of His Word is generic, and the truth of salvation is generic—meant for all, true for all, everlasting life for all. In this specific truth we are saved: Christ bore our sins and died on the cross—one death, one resurrection—for all. Then it is the specific truth He speaks over our personal circumstances and situations that allows us to walk out in fruitfulness. It's the *personal* truth from Him that fills us with the strength and courage to follow His will. This is *exactly* the time when we walk out the freedom and liberty we have gained from our new identities and restoration.

Recently, I discovered I had what is called "leaky gut." It's a condition in which the gut lining has holes in it, and what is meant to stay in leaks out. The term that doctors would use to properly describe this is *increased permeability*. I am so grateful for the information I found and the book I used to pretty much heal it, *Eat Dirt*, by Dr. Josh Axe. In the book he reminds us of the old phrase "You are what you eat." He corrects that line of thinking with something more accurate: "You are what you can absorb." In the leaky gut example, this is 100 per cent true. I had been having gut issues and been taking several supplements for years. Not until this year did I understand why nothing was helping or working. I had to heal the lining of my gut before I could count on things being absorbed and doing any good for me.

When we talk about faith, I'd like to use the same line of thinking. The truth of God is only as good in our lives as what we can absorb and internalize. Reading and knowing are of no use if we cannot make it real. We need to be healed and then use the truth to change our minds and hearts. The truth *must* be manifested, made real, and made relevant in our lives for it to lead us to victory.

Why say all this? Why bother to go through the exercise of dissecting truth? Because life is hard. And sometimes truth is all we seek. The enemy will have us believing lies in the blink of an eye. Situations can be overwhelming and very scary. The enemy loves to tell us we can't handle it. Just yesterday I was dealing with some heavy stuff. I was shaking for a while and crying while I was driving. I continued to talk to God about it, and in the end, this is what I came up with: "Lord, I know you have me. I know you have my husband. And I know you have each one of my children in the palm of your hand. You care for us all, and we are cherished by you. You know all things. I don't have to carry this; you are carrying me."

Tears streamed down my face because of the validity I felt and the happiness at being able to say that but, more importantly at *knowing* and being able to *rely* on those truths. My head was nodding up and down, because I felt God agreeing with me. It was as if He were there, riding shotgun and saying, "Yes, Tammy, I do."

God's truth grounds us so we can do this thing called life. It's difficult enough sometimes. I cannot imagine going through it without

Him. Far too many people do, and it's sad. He wants nothing more than to be with us every step of the way.

My wish is that each one of you know more truth and walk out each day holding the hand of the biggest and bestest daddy of all time. Know the truth; know His truth. Know your truth from Him alone. If you lack some specific kind of truth in your life, then seek till you find it. Ask. Pray. Listen. If you do, you will find it. You will find *Him*.

CHAPTER 4

Identity Crisis

HERE IS THE READING FROM LUKE AGAIN. *"THEN THEY sailed to the country of the Gadarenes, which is opposite Galilee. And when he stepped out on the land, there met Him a certain man from the city who had demons for a long time. And he wore no clothes, nor did he live in house, but in tombs. When he saw Jesus, he cried out, fell down before Him and with a loud voice said, 'What have I to do with you, Jesus, Son of the Most High God? I beg you do not torment me' ... then they went out to see what had happened, and came to Jesus, and found the man from whom the demons had departed, sitting at the feet of Jesus, clothed and in his right mind."*

Let's look at this passage to incorporate another principal that has been integral in my life and key to the man in the story too—identity. I'd like to note that Jesus not only restored his mind and freed him but *what* he restored was his identity. In my walk with God, the single biggest blessing I ever received and accepted (other than salvation) is from 2 Corinthians 5:17: *"Therefore, if anyone is in Christ, he is a new creation; old things have passed away, behold, all things have become new."* The day I heard this scripture, I was forever changed! I had been aching to be freed from my past and hungry for a new beginning. God gave me that.

It has been said that it is impossible to incorporate the Word of God in our lives and not be changed. How true—how true! When we accept Jesus as Lord and Saviour we have access to the life-changing truth at its core. I remember the day when I heard this scripture being discussed. That very day I accepted it as truth, and from that moment I allowed it to be true for me.

I believe the truth that reveals our identities to us can be the single most powerful truth of our lives—or the one that brings the most devastation! Once we accept our identities as daughters or sons of God—royalty, really—we can be free from the notion that other people can tell us who we are. Nor can circumstances affect us to the core. Like deep water that never changes, regardless of the storm or calm on the surface, this truth takes us to the penetrating peace of God that is unchanging, unwavering, and non-exhaustive.

Truthfully, this topic seems to be at the heart of most of the talking I do with people these days. Not everyone is ready to hear, but the concept is that we are not our circumstances, not our pasts, not our illnesses, and so on, but that we are created in Him and that our truest identity is inward, not outward.

When we accept Jesus as Lord and Saviour, we get a fresh, clean start. How fabulous is this? It absolutely changed my life! Friend, accepting this truth can free you from so much heavy, unwanted baggage. The joy in knowing that the past does not dictate the future—well, for some of you that's enough right there! I mean, just going with that would change what you did tomorrow and every day afterward, because it would change what you think. What a most wonderful paradigm shift this is! Thus the people who told you that you were stupid were wrong. The abusive home you grew up in doesn't have to be all you know. The alcoholic parent didn't set the best example for you—more accurately, the alcoholic parent was the *worst* example in your life—but it was all you knew. Now there's another example. You can be pure, cherished, and beautiful, despite the childhood molestation, abuse, or neglect you might have suffered. There is healing and freedom and joy and peace and all the restoration your heart has always wanted. Your identity does not have to reflect the things you lived through, the devastation you knew, or the pain you hid for years.

Your identity is in Him. Rested. Renewed. Full of hope and peace. Yes, it really is. Perhaps this is new and you're just processing this information. Perhaps rested and renewed hasn't happened yet? That's okay. It can. It will. What you need to know, is not *who* you are but *Whose* you are. I am in no way saying that those of you who had a wonderful childhood should miss out on anything here. What I am saying is that every single one of us needs to know Who we belong to. I think because my story came from pain, not peace, that I just started there. I know a lot of you can relate. If you can't relate, I'm sure you know someone who can.

Our identity in Him is crucial as we move forward. The distractions around us compete for not only our attention but for our hearts as well. John 10:10 says, *"The thief does not come except to steal, and to kill, and to destroy."* What do you think he comes to steal? He comes to steal our joy and our inheritance by lying to us about who we really are (among other things, of course). He does not have to take our physical lives to kill us, just keep us from comprehending this principle, wear us down enough so we turn our hearts away from Jesus. Don't let that happen. Understand this principle, it is part of the truth that sets us free.

Imagine, if you will, trying to get on a plane with a ticket that has your name on it but you're using someone else's ID? It would be impossible, right? They'd stop you right at the gate and escort you out. Well, once we have the salvation of Christ, we are full of Him. We become heirs to the throne, princes and princesses. Picture yourself with a crown and know you belong to the King. We are, therefore, a new creation (back to 2 Corinthians 5:17).

The problem lies where you have the identity of someone else— your *old* (perhaps broken) self. When you take on an identity that is other than Christ-centred, you lose the freedom that goes with it. The ticket you are holding to victorious living is only good with the right identity. Circumstances don't matter. The past doesn't matter. Other people's opinions don't matter. What does matter is what God says about you. This can be an incredibly liberating concept. Some of you are stuck *on* something or stuck *in* something that holds you back. The reality is that you aren't just being held back, you're paralyzed and unable to live. I get it. That happened to me, too. That can stop here and now; accept this gift and walk forward like the royalty you really are.

We need to be very careful of the things we say about ourselves, the things we self-profess in relation to our hearts. As I mentioned before, I was saved as an adult. Everything I learned in my early Christian walk was a new and dramatic experience; it literally changed me. When I came to God, I was a mess. I had a myriad of issues, which were in some way identities for me, and they were all holding me captive each in their own way.

We tend to "own" our circumstances and wear them like clothes. The divorced woman feels outcast. The neglected teen supresses anger and can't imagine real love. The cancer survivor feels tired and worn, and the person who suffered a tragedy recently may lose all confidence in life and people. It becomes a very slippery slope when we focus on the tangible events as "us," as "normal" and "real." The divorced woman is not outcast; she is cherished by the Most High God. The teen is the apple of God's eye. The cancer survivor is not just a survivor but "more than a conqueror." The people going through tragedies are fashioned by the creator of the universe and put in exactly the right time and place. He knows every detail of our lives. We are all written on the palm of His hand. What is real is that we are inheriting the Kingdom. Wear your crowns proudly!

Wrong identities hold us captive. My life changed drastically the day I believed He made me new, the day I accepted the better things he had to offer. Note the word *accepted*. Jesus gives us a new identity. He gives us freedom and restoration and peace. We must be active in receiving and accepting these things. I stand on knowing that I don't have to let the things of the past identify me. The past is not the future. I continue to learn and grow into the things He says I am. If you would be willing to trade God some of your haunting identities, He would be thrilled to hand you something better. (Isaiah 43:16, 18–19)

Mark 12:30 says, *"Love the Lord your God with all your heart, with all your soul, with all your mind, and with all your strength."* The things that hold us captive take up space in our hearts and minds and use up our strength. If we would be willing to trade God some beauty for ashes (Isaiah 61:3) we would have more room in our hearts for love, more space in our minds to love, and more strength in our wills to ... yes, love. I say love because it simply comes down to that. When we are hurting, our hearts tend to close a bit. Our minds fill with thoughts that don't do us any good. Our strength is used fighting the thoughts and bad feelings. We end up stuck, and times of pain can seem to go on and on. When we are hurting, we want to feel better, but some of us have been going about it the wrong way. Instead of looking out, or back, we need to look up.

We need to be willing to consider that what we've been doing isn't working. Some of us may struggle with this concept. We're not in trouble and we haven't done anything wrong. Well, not on purpose anyway. Nobody really says to themselves, "I want to stay in agony, and I am going to cling to my negative life events and circumstances like a blanket." Yet that's exactly what happens. On whatever level and in whatever dire or simply negative circumstances, we are kind of wired to use past events and experiences to guide us emotionally and instinctively. What I am suggesting is that we take on our new identities and relearn who we are. We can undo the negative, self-abusive words we use. We can rethink the purpose and dreams we have accepted about ourselves. Our new identities can take us places we never thought possible—this is not pretend! It's not like wearing a mask and acting like someone else. I am talking about the authentic, beautiful, unabashed, and amazing ability to live the way we were meant to—free, whole, and abundant.

What we must do, and it's an instant decision, is to accept. Simply say, "Yes, Lord, I believe you. I believe that where I have been and what I have done do not dictate who I am. You do. You made me, and I accept that I am yours. I accept that the moment I gave myself to you, you made me new, and I don't need to wear these ugly old clothes anymore. Today, we start fresh." Say that out loud, and smile. Let it sink in.

Lay It Down

We need to be willing to leave some junk on the altar. He will take *all* of it if we will relinquish it to Him. We need to be willing to unburden ourselves from the opinions of others and the scars of the self-inflicted wounds of our bad decisions and self-talk. It sounds hard, but isn't that what we all really want, deep down? I challenge you today to be willing to accept your identity in Christ in its fullness. Begin to walk in a new light and with real strength, knowing that the Maker of the universe lives inside of you!

I will be brutally honest here. I left on the altar the parts of me that were abused, bitter, afraid, misunderstood, lonely, broken, neglected, criticized, ashamed, guilty, and enslaved. I accepted from God in replacement of those things new features that are now part of my identity: a protected me, a humbled me, a restored me, the accepted-and-loved-for-who-I-am me, the Daughter of the King me, the divinely loved me, the healed me, the renewed me, the beautifully designed me, the forgiven me, the whole me, and the saved me. Now, keep in mind that the list is fluid, and He adds to it as we walk out my life. As children of God, friends, we are not made for mediocrity, not created for criticism, nor are we meant to live without knowing, receiving, and being blessed in the promises of God.

Until I was willing to let God give me a new identity, I would always be the victim of something or other. I was broken as broken could be when I met Him. We traded old for new, beauty for ashes. I believe we all have something we would like to leave behind. As I mentioned before, this may be a good time to start writing. What should we give Him? I've been very personal; I gave some real examples. I always believed my pain was for someone else's gain. That time is now. Isaiah 61:3 says, *"To console those who mourn in Zion, to give them beauty for ashes, the oil of joy for mourning, the garment of praise for the spirit of heaviness, that they may be called trees of righteousness, the planting of the Lord, that He may be glorified."* I have referred to this scripture many times in the past few pages for a reason. Let it sink in. Let it be your whole new truth.

Letting go of your old self allows you to go deeper in your commitment and relationship with Him. Isaiah 55:9 says, *"For as the heavens are higher than the earth, so are My ways higher than your ways, and My thoughts than your thoughts."* Use this truth to allow His thoughts about you to transcend what you know about yourself. It doesn't matter what you may or may not be going through. You may not be stuck at this point in your life. I'm asking, though, that you look deeply within yourself and your heart. Be truthful about the guard you may have up and the hurts you may be keeping out. Know this: a guard is not a filter; it is a block. Like chemotherapy drugs that kill all cells, good and bad, a heart block keeps out the love we desperately desire along with the hurt we are trying to avoid. This thought may bring a moment of insight for you. This truth can give you a fresh breath of the life He has already breathed into you. God is inviting you to trade with Him that which hurts for that which is beautiful! You might use Galatians 5:22–23 as a measuring stick. *"But the fruit of the Spirit is love, joy, peace, longsuffering [patience through suffering], kindness, goodness, faithfulness, gentleness, self-control."* As we trade old for new, beauty for ashes, death for life, we embody these attributes more and more. Yes, it really happens.

A new identity allows you to be justified by His grace. It is written in Romans 3:23–24, *"For all have sinned and fall short of the glory of God, being justified freely by His grace through the redemption that is Jesus Christ."*

Take a few minutes and ask God for those things He can replace in your identity that would bring him honour and bring you closer to Him. Write down one or as many things as you would like to give over to Him. These might be things that have hurt you, things that have happened, or things other people have imposed on you. Some examples are abuse of some sort, rape, divorce, disease, criticism, neglect, or sin. Use things you would describe yourself as or a way someone else may describe you. Use descriptive words by saying "I feel ..." or this big one, "I am ..." Once you will it to Him, he will begin a work in you. You may use some of the examples that I shared to help, if you identify with them. It is also just as important to write down what you want in return. Take your time. You will know. God wants you to have it.

The purpose of this book is victorious living. Breaking free is hard work! I never promised an easy read. There are plenty of magazines that can offer you that. I have one goal: giving you tools that will allow you to live free in Him. This is the hardest part of the book, but I promise it's worth every minute of tears and agony when you allow Him to release you from those haunting memories and pain that have no right to be there.

Once you have made a mental list (or better yet a list on paper) of some of the parts of your identity you are leaving on His altar, along with the things you wish to receive from him—like acceptance or unconditional love—you can begin to use the new identities and truths to create powerful statements about yourself. Said out loud these can absolutely change your days. They are like weapons when the enemy tries to remind you of what or who you were. They are called "I am" statements. "I am" statements help you proclaim the newness and truth of the great identity you have in Christ. Remember, there is a universal truth at work here—whatever you focus on you get more of! Too many of us (particularly those who have gone through/are going through very trying circumstances) focus on how hard things are, how much things hurt, and how frustrated we are. This only draws more of the same. Learning to focus on "do-want thinking" versus "don't-want thinking" will bring more of His blessings. A book I have read explains this so well. It is called *Promptings*, and it's by Kody Bateman (founder of SendOutCards). The book helped me formulate my "I am" statements to help me speak out loud the new and radical parts of me that are true, and at the same time really understand how toxic "don't-want thinking" can be. Scripture says we "must be transformed by the renewing of our minds" (Romans 12:2) and this is simply part of it.

Focusing on being open to receive more of Him will bring, well, *more* of Him. Using "I am" statements can shift our thoughts to something better and, more importantly, align us with God's thoughts toward us. We can never know God's thoughts (Isaiah 40:28, Romans 11:34). But we can learn what He says about us and choose not only to believe it but to profess it, using the "I am" statements that we have been talking about. They go like this:

I am free, liberated from my circumstances and sin.
    I am unconditionally loved and protected by my heavenly Father.
        I am forgiven, justified, and redeemed by Christ's death for me.
            I am beautiful and cherished just as I am.
                I am a princess, a daughter of the king, heir to the throne.

Now fill in a few of your own:
I am _____
I am _____
I am _____
I am _____
I am _____

Doesn't that feel good? Isn't it time you were a bit nicer to yourself? Again, this may not have hit all of you over the head the way it did me. But I know it will be an exercise you can remind someone else of. We all know someone who aches to be unconditionally loved, or accepted at the very least, and this exercise allows us to show them how to find this love.

I can guarantee that when we recognize and accept our pure identities in Christ, understand *Whose* we are, and what an amazing God we belong to, we will begin to see others differently too. True understanding of this prevents judgement against others, or at least it should. The homeless person is loved just as you are. The poor, the widows, the well-to-dos, and the not-so-well-to-dos have the same access to the same identity in the same God. Identity in Christ levels the playing field of life.

What will follow is the ability to see from a whole new perspective. If we understand this truth in our own lives, we will then be more able to recognize the lack of freedom in others. Instead of walking around offended, we will then have the ability to live and act, from a place of love. Knowing who and whose we are, and understanding our identities, will allow us to have mercy on those around us, because that's what we will be covered in. I found that once this truth penetrated my consciousness, my purpose shifted. And I saw people in a whole new way. This poem sums it up.

Overflowing

My heart is overflowing today
With dreams,
And joy,
And peace.
I feel as though
I've crossed the line
That held me back,
Burst through the ceiling
That held me down,
Released the boulder from my shoulders,

Threw off the lid of the box
I've been living in.

I now see a big, beautiful world,
And I feel as though
I can reach across the ocean
And touch a soul.
I used to be afraid,
But now I am not,
Of the far-reaching world.

I'm was even afraid of me, sometimes,
Afraid to dream and long and want
For more.
But now
I am new,
I am free,
To give and receive
Love
 —Tammy Tassone, 2013

Prayer

Awesome God, Lord over all,
I love You with all my surrendered heart.
You made me, and You don't make mistakes.
I am wonderfully made by Your loving hands, have purpose and hope in You;
Because I love You, and because You made me, and because You live in me, I can love myself.
I accept that You love me, and I accept *Your* beauty for *my* ashes.
I thank You with all my heart.
I will honour my heart with Your hand and help;
I will live free from the pain of the past, with Your forgiveness of me, and with forgiveness of myself—these allow me to forgive others and set them free because of the love You have shown me.
I will walk into tomorrow with hope and joy, because You are with me every step of the way.

Lord, thank you for my identity in You.
I am loved and cherished by You; that is really all I need.
You are my King.
Continue to wipe away the fog, Lord, so that I may see clearly who I really am, so that I may be used by You in this beautiful world.
Amen

CHAPTER 5

Restoration

ACTUAL RESTORATION REFERS TO "THE ACT OF restoring or the condition of being restored; to bring back to a former condition or restore to an unimpaired condition." We are talking about the latter. Salvation restores us to God and brings us back to Him. This restoration ensures eternal life in heaven. What we are talking about in this book is the restoration Jesus gives us through His truth and His death and resurrection. The goal is daily victorious living, and it is only through the restoration of and from Jesus that we can accomplish this. Salvation brings us to Him. *Restoration binds us to the glory we can have here on earth*—so we don't have to wait for eternity to have victory.

It is clear from the scriptures we are focusing on (found at the beginning of this book) that many people came to Jesus to be healed. There were those who were possessed by evil spirits, those who needed healing from diseases, and those who asked for healing from death. From these readings, we clearly see that we can depend on God for our life, both physical and spiritual and also for physical and spiritual healing. The physical need is easy to identify, visualize, and understand. When we see people sick or with a broken leg, for example, we can absolutely understand the need for healing. Being sick undoubtedly keeps us from living our best days. We all know people who are threatened with life-taking illnesses and diseases. Their plea for more time on this earth is understandable too. The family members of those who are threatened raise up many prayers for healing. We want our family members around us, to spend more time with us and to live out more of their lives.

The other kind of healing people go to God for is the kind we usually cannot see; it is spiritual healing, including forgiveness. I believe that when we are broken, it is one of the most critical times we meet with God. We become broken over and over. I mean, let's face it, we are imperfect beings. We have a clean slate in salvation through God's forgiveness. Yet our humanness guarantees that we will absolutely sin again. The need for forgiveness is ongoing, and we should be aware of this and aware too, that we can have it. Sometimes, though, we don't seek it. Why? I am sure that embarrassment, regret, and shame are smokescreens that keep us hiding in our pain, especially when we have committed an outward sin. The enemy works hard to keep us in the dark, to keep us out of the light, locked and bound in our own secret chains. If we don't seek the redemption that we need, we will be rendered ineffective for Christ for as long a time as we wallow in that misery. For some people that time will be short, while for others, years may pass. The enemy knows this, and so in the spiritual battle we wage it is one of the easiest tactics he knows. It is imperative then, that we seek forgiveness and freedom from this bondage *immediately*! I like to think of it like this: if you cut your hand, you would probably put on some ointment to stop infection and cover it with a bandage. After a few days of ointment and clean bandages, you would leave the bandage off, expose the cut to air, and let it heal that way. If you kept it covered and moist, it would not heal properly, and it would take much longer. So it is with our broken hearts that need healing. We tend to cover up the hurt feelings, brokenness, and sin, and we sometimes keep them covered for far too long. We need to expose them to the air: repent, pray, and ask God for help. Remember, secrecy keeps us in chains. Keeping sin or hurts covered insures they don't heal. Air heals. Exposing it to the light is the only way. The cut may sting and be unprotected and vulnerable, but exposure really is the only way. And so it is with us. We need the light of Christ, to be shone on us so we can be healed.

Right now, as you've been reading, you may have recognized a specific circumstance that you have been keeping a secret. Ask God to shine His light all over the situation and ask Him for the forgiveness He so longs to give you. Again, use the margin to write down those things that you believe may be sins or a secret shame you need help with.

The scriptures also show us family members who begged Jesus to heal their loved ones. We need to be courageous enough to bring to Him our family members who have spiritual problems. The people in the stories here had some very serious things going on, like "unclean spirits." For most of us, this won't be the battle we wage. Our battles will be for spirits of depression, anxiety, fear, worthlessness, and hate, among others. The wars we fight will tend to be silent and unseen. The broken leg is easy to spot; the broken heart is not. Depression and anxiety are silent killers in our modern society. There are more broken hearts around us than we know. There are true battles going on in our families. Children are being gripped by feelings of worthlessness and fear; spouses are fighting with resentment and cold, shut-down hearts because of the lies of comparison; others are watching their loved ones fight alcohol and drug abuse in record numbers. And we all fit in somewhere—in some cases all of those scenarios.

Jesus is a restorative Lord. Jesus is *the* restoration we have been searching for in so many other things. Intercessory prayer may not have been your thing, but when your teenager spirals out of control with depression or drugs, your knees may hurt from being on them saying prayers you never thought possible. We need to be aware that we can go to God for anything. *Anything!* Yes, we can pour our hearts out in our agony, but we can also seek and claim healing for our loved ones. Please note I did not just say *ask*. I said *claim*.

Be so desperate that you are willing to lower them in through the roof! (Mark 2: 3–5) Let us be so vigilant as parents, siblings, and friends. Let us be unrelenting in our prayers to Jesus for the restoration and healing of our loved ones with spiritual sickness. He is the true restorer. He also intercedes for us to the Father. We must know this is what He does. "Stand on what you know" is advice I give out constantly. It applies here, too. And what about us? What happens when *we* are the ones who are sick? Without the broken leg, who will see? How can anyone know we are sick, especially when we don't tell anyone? Some of us live in quiet pain for years. We smile and keep it in. We keep it pressed down and covered up like the sore with the bandage on it. What's wrong in pretending, anyway? Nobody needs to know; it's our own business, right?

When we wear masks to make sure nobody knows our hurt, it is like a double-edged sword. We don't want people to know, yet we are silently screaming for someone to save us. *Keeping the secret is the enemy's idea.* He wants us to stay stuck in our junk; if we don't tell, we probably won't be saved from it. But Jesus cares. He knows and wants to heal us. He can find us even when we are hiding. Does the reading from Luke regarding the man who lived in the tombs sound familiar? Did you ever hear or say yourself, "I just want to crawl under a rock"? He did live under a rock, literally. He had no friends around to pray for him. You need to know that even if you are alone there is hope. There is freedom from the darkness. There is restoration.

Assurances of Restoration

When we talk about restoration, we must also consider redemption. When looking at the difference between the two, restoration and redemption, we are splitting hairs; it's the process we need to differentiate. *Redemption* is instant and immediate. Jesus's death on the cross accomplished this. I suppose one could stop here. There's a huge question mark for me though. *Why* would someone stop here? Why wouldn't anyone who got to this point not want restoration? That's the part that puts us back together! Yet this is where I meet so many people who are stuck, stuck, stuck. It takes courage to acknowledge your junk and be willing to lay it down. Personally, I should think we would be willing to throw it all away.

Restoration can sometimes be a time-consuming, painstaking, pour-all-the-love-you-have-into-it kind of project. But God loves us so much He is willing to put in the time and energy; we just need to let Him. Isaiah 64:8 says, *"Yet you, Lord, are our Father, we are the clay, you are the potter; we are all the work of your hand."* Probably more popular is the verse from Jeremiah 18:3–4: *"Then I went down to the potter's house, and there he was, making something at the wheel. And the vessel that he made of clay was marred in the hand of the potter; so he made it again into another vessel, as it seemed good to the potter to make."*

Let's look now at the guarantees we have in allowing God to restore us.

Salvation (past, once for all)

The work of Jesus on the cross accomplished this. His death and resurrection mean you have access to a new life, a new beginning, a new heart, a clean slate.

1 Peter 3:18
For Christ also suffered once for sins, the just for the unjust, that He might bring us to God, being put to death in the flesh but made alive by the Spirit.

Romans 10:8–10
The word is near you, in your mouth and in your heart, (that is, the word of faith which we preach): that if you confess with your mouth "Jesus is

Lord" and believe in your heart that God has raised him from the dead, you will be saved. For with the heart one believes unto righteousness, and with the mouth confession is made unto salvation.

John 3:16
For God so loved the world that he gave his one and only Son, that whoever believes in him shall not perish but have everlasting life.

John 14:6
Jesus said to him, "I am the way, the truth, and the life. No one comes to the Father except through me."

John 3:3, 5–7
Jesus replied, "Very truly I tell you, no one can enter the kingdom of God unless they are born of water and the Spirit. Flesh gives birth to flesh, but the Spirit gives birth to spirit. You should not be surprised at my saying, 'You must be born again.'"

Salvation (present and ongoing)

1 John 1:7
But if we walk in the light as He is in the light, we have fellowship with one another, and the blood of Jesus Christ his Son cleanses us from all sin.

Psalm 51:7–12
Purge me with hyssop, and I shall be clean; Wash me and I shall be whiter than snow. Make me hear joy and gladness, that the bones You have broken may rejoice. Hide your face from my sins, and blot out all my iniquities. Create in me a clean heart, O God, and renew a steadfast spirit within me.

Psalm 62:7
In God is my salvation and my glory, the rock of my strength, and my refuge is in God.

2 Peter 3:9
The Lord is not slack concerning His promise, as some count slackness, but is longsuffering toward us, not willing that any should perish but that all should come to repentance.

Through the salvation of God, we are saved (once and ongoing); because of the justification of God, we are justified (once and ongoing). Through the redemption of God, we are redeemed (once and ongoing); by the sanctification of God we are sanctified (once and ongoing).

Eternal Life

John 10:28–30
And I give them eternal life, and they shall never perish; neither shall anyone snatch them out of My hand. My Father, who has given them to Me, is greater than all; and no one is able to snatch them out of My Fathers hand, I and My Father are one.

John 3:15–17
That everyone who believes may have eternal life in Him. For God so loved the world that he gave his one and only Son, that whoever believes in him shall not perish but have eternal life. For God did not send his son into the world to condemn the world, but to save the world through Him.

Redemption

1 Peter 1:18–19
Knowing that you were not redeemed with corruptible things, like silver or gold, from your aimless conduct received by tradition from your fathers but with the precious blood of Christ, as a lamb without blemish ad without spot.

Romans 3:23–24
For all have sinned and fall short of the glory of God, being justified by His grace through the redemption that is in Jesus Christ.

Forgiveness

Psalm 86:5
For you, Lord, are good, and ready to forgive, and abundant in mercy to all those who call upon you.

Psalm 65:3
When we were overwhelmed by sins, you forgave our transgressions.

Matthew 26:28
For this is My blood of the new covenant, which is shed for many for the remission of sins.

1 John 1:9
If we confess our sins, He is faithful and just to forgive us our sins and to cleanse us from all unrighteousness.

Acts 10:43
To Him all the prophets witness that, through His name, whoever believes in Him -will receive remission of sins.

Acts 13:38–39
Therefore, let it be known to you, brethren, that through this Man is preached to you the forgiveness of sins; and by Him everyone who believes is justified from all things from which you could not be justified by the law of Moses.

Ephesians 1:7
In Him we have redemption through His blood, the forgiveness of sins, according to the riches of His grace.

Freedom

LIKE TRUTH, FREEDOM IS ALSO MULTI-LAYERED, AS ARE the truths we seek. We have the freedom of salvation; it is our ticket to heaven, so to speak. Yet this truth does not mean that we will live happy lives. The truth we allow God to speak over us through prayer and discernment is the ammunition we need to then live 'more freely on our road to "freedom." *This, friends, is victorious living—a daily walk in freedom with God!* Perhaps, too, I should say that freedom does not mean that the lives we mentioned earlier don't exist anymore. Being in a deep and connected relationship with God does not ensure a euphoric state of life. It does not mean hearts don't get broken and we don't suffer loss or grief or sadness. It means that when we go through those things, we have Him to count on, to lean on, and to bear it all to. I can't imagine going through the pains of life without Him.

It could easily be said that the opposite of freedom is slavery. What, then, causes us to be enslaved? We have been talking about this throughout the book, because the awareness of the things that entrap our hearts and minds is of utter importance. In fact, our lives depend on it. Why? It's because those are the things that yoke us. They are, therefore, the things that Jesus came to set us free from. Commonly, we need to be freed from ourselves. The paradigm is a shift from flesh to spirit, from tangible to perceived, from outer to inner. Yes, as we walk it out (our faith and purpose), we become tangible and outward witnesses in the world, but it must start in our hearts and on our lips! Friends, restoration and identity in Christ Jesus allow us access to freedom, freedom from many kinds of bondages. What's your story? I have shared much of mine, hoping that you who ache to be free will have the courage to do it. Hopefully, those of you who are in a great place can recognize the need in others. May we always be the hands and feet of our Lord when called. And of course, yes, we will be talking about this, too. God wants us to have freedom in our freedom!

Romans 8:1–2
Therefore, there is now no condemnation for those who are in Christ Jesus, because through Christ Jesus the law of the Spirit who gives life has set you free from the law of sin and death.

Jesus does, however, also free us from oppressive situations and people. The entire book of Exodus explains this, and I won't go into it more. Our personal situations are what I am focusing on, and they are significantly meaningful to Him.

Psalm 146:7
He upholds the cause of the oppressed and gives food to the hungry. The Lord sets prisoners free.

Isaiah 58:6
Is this not the kind of fasting I have chosen: to loose the chains of injustice and untie the cords of the yoke, to set the oppressed free and break every yoke.

My very favourite on personal freedom is this.

Jeremiah 29:11–1
For you know the plans I have for you, declares the Lord, "plans to prosper you and not to harm you, plans to give you hope and a future. Then you will call on me and come and pray to me and I will listen to you. You will seek me and find me when you seek me with all your heart, I will be found by you," declares the Lord, *"and will bring you back from captivity, I will gather you from all the nations and places where I have banished you,"* declares the Lord, *"and will bring you back to the place from which I carried you into exile."* I've spoken of this scripture before. There's just so much in it. We referenced it earlier concerning the way He hears us. This time I am talking about His desire to retrieve us out of captivity. What might that mean to you right now? Everywhere I go, I find people stressed, full of anxiety, and wrapped up in fear of tomorrow and the future. I talk to people who love God, yet they are bound in chains of

disbelief. They are skeptical and unbelieving about His will toward their lives and His willingness to share with them His forgiveness, peace, rest, and mercy. So, let's go on to those.

Jesus knows how much we need his love. He doesn't just save us and leave us to figure it out. He stays and makes sure we have a way—*the Way*. The way is Him. I found myself praying recently, "Lord, show me the way." I was working through a problem, and I needed Him to guide me. I realized right as I said it that His Way is an all-day-every-day, come-to-me, I-wanna-help-you-through-every-detail kind of help. *Jesus has not come to offer salvation alone, but He has come to offer us a way through Him to have victory daily!* This offering is an incredible and beautiful act, second only to Him giving up His life for us.

Surrendering to Him, allowing our hurts to be exposed to His light, and then following His lead to where the healing really is, is the only way to have true and lasting freedom. If you're anything like me, you have a list of things you know you need to deal with. One of the amazingly wonderful aspects of God is how much of a gentleman He is; this means He will be gentle with your junk, and He won't leave you. Restoration, friends, is on its way. We all have the capacity to be new and improved persons! But we must be sure to allow the one true healer in on our list and let Him do His thing.

Peace

Jesus said in John 14:27, *"Peace I leave with you; my peace I give to you. I do not give you as the world gives. Do not let your hearts be troubled and do not be afraid."* He offers freely. Why don't we take it? I learned several years ago that happiness is an inside job. When we make our happiness conditional on tangible things, we enter into agreements that are outside of God and His purposes.

Don't let your peace be subject to external conditions, such as status, finances, education, home, or any other "comfort" you may seek that meets your criteria or outwardly shows you "have it together." God works diligently with you to ensure this is a concept you understand in word and in your heart. I prayed for patience seventeen years ago and was blessed with twin boys. True story. How many of you laughed? Well, if you've prayed for peace, I will bet you've been thrown some circumstances that challenged it! That's the way it works. What we get are opportunities to cultivate the things we desire, such as peace, for instance. Isaiah 26:3 says, *"You will keep him in perfect peace, whose mind is stayed on you, because he trusts in You."* So look not outward but upward for your peace. Be of God's good courage to not fall into temptation, worry, and lose your peace. Matthew 6:27 asks *"Which one of you by worrying can add one cubit to his stature?"* Perhaps you should try to pay attention the next time you hear yourself say, "I am worried about/because ...." Take that opportunity to give it to God and move on. I am by no means diminishing the things we can be concerned about. Honestly, right now I have a biggie, a situation that could keep me up all night. I am learning how to lean in to God and let Him handle it—just saying.

Philippians 4:7 tells us, *"And the peace of God, which surpasses all understanding, will guard your hearts and minds through Christ Jesus."*

Then there is Romans 15:13: *"May the God of hope fill you with all joy and peace as you trust in him, so that you may overflow with hope by the power of the Holy Spirit."*

I especially love this next one, because we have been speaking of restoration. Not only does this verse talk about peace, it urges us to seek full restoration. Guess what? That's where peace can be found. When we have internal strife (the goal of the enemy) we will have a hard time having peace. *"Finally, brothers and sisters, rejoice! Strive for full restoration, encourage one another, be of one mind, live in peace. And the God of love and peace will be with you."* (2 Corinthians 13:11)

Colossians 3:15 says, *"And let the peace of God rule in your hearts, to which you were also called in one body; and be thankful."* Not only should peace rule the space in our hearts, it should rule as a guide.

Think about it. I know it makes sense to you, but rarely do people operate on this level. When they have a decision to make, what do most people do? They think about it. Firstly, that's a bad idea, because our minds cannot be trusted; they are full of fears, ideas, concepts, judgements, experiences, and all kinds of irrational things. The Holy Spirit dispenses peace when we are on the right track, and we can feel it, right in our guts. I heard it described like this by a wonderful teaching recently: "I know as I know in my knower." We all have a "knower" in the pit of our stomach; that is the discernment centre we should all strive to cultivate. Essentially, it is peace.

Getting back to the decision, consider one of the choices in your mind, and if you don't feel peace in your "knower," then it's wrong. If, on the other hand, you do feel peace, then that's the choice God could be leading you to. Of course, prayer should have immediately preceded the process. If you don't believe me, give it a whirl. Don't take my word for it; take God's. Listen to Him. Let Him nudge you and fill you with unmistakable peace. Just go with it.

Rest

Knowing that God gives us rest, I am able to lay a lot of things down. Sometimes this truth is the only reason I can truly, truly rest. Once I have poured out my heart and it's in His hands, I can relax. He calls us to rest in Him; the invitation is constant and open.

Matthew 11:28–29 advises, *"Come to me, all you who labor and are heavy laden, and I will give you rest. Take my yoke upon you and learn from me, for I am gentle and lowly in heart and you will find rest for your souls."* What I love about this is that we don't have to do it on our own strength; we get to enter into His presence, where there is rest. We get His, from Him. It's perfect in every way. Many of us strive to find times and places to rest. We mistake putting our feet up for unburdening our souls.

In Exodus 33:14, *"The Lord replied, 'My Presence will go with you, and I will give you rest.'"*

Psalm 23:1–3 repeats the same theme: *"The Lord is my shepherd; I shall not want; He makes me to lie down in green pastures; He leads me beside the still waters. He restores my soul; He leads me in the paths of righteousness For His name's sake."* While the verse does not specifically say "rest," we know that this is what David is talking about. Depending on the version you use, it may use the word *rest*. The point is that God leads us to rest when we follow Him. Well, at least He can if we are willing to lay down our junk. It's exhausting doing things on our own strength, in our own way, and with our own timing. Doing things God's way and in His timing is so much easier! This particular scripture not only talks about rest, but it wraps it up with peace and mercy, too. How wonderful!

In Jeremiah 6:16 we read, *"Thus says the Lord; 'Stand in the ways and see, and ask for the old paths, where the good way is, and walk in it; then you will find rest for you souls.'"* From Old Testament to New, God promises us rest. Go to Him. Jump into His arms. Give Him your junk. Pour it out. He can handle it.

It is also true and to be expected that lessons of faith and dependence require time. In a world of instant gratification, the concept of waiting can be frustrating. Yet the lessons of waiting are everywhere in the Bible. David is one of the best examples. He waited twenty-two years before being crowned king after being told at the age of fifteen that he would be. How many things in your life require you to just wait? The waiting God is referring to does not just mean expecting your turn or being lazy and absent. It infers faith and trust and surrender. Psalm 27:13–14 says, *"I would have lost heart, unless I had believed that I would see the goodness of the Lord in the land of the living. Wait on the Lord; be of good courage and he shall strengthen your heart; wait, I say, on the Lord!"*

CHAPTER 6

Lead the Way

DEPENDENCE ON GOD FOR GUIDANCE IS A WAY OF LIFE and, like breathing, must become second nature. Matthew 6:33 tells us, *"But seek first the Kingdom of God and His righteousness, and all these things shall be added to you."* The scripture is referring to food, clothing, and the necessities of life. When we depend on Him all day, every day, we will be amazed at how things work for our good (Romans 8:28). We need to count on Him for everything we do in our days, for all our decisions, and for all the strength to make the decisions we know He is leading us to. He must be our constant and limitless source, for without this we disconnect, if even for a little while. I say "limitless" because that is exactly what He is; but more than that, He is exactly what we need. We need a power source that never ends, a power source that doesn't quit at five, one that is constant, no matter what the time of day or circumstances under which we need it. The more we depend, the more we stay close and are connected. Thus it follows that the *less* we depend, the further away and disconnected we will be. You cannot disconnect a plug from the outlet and expect things to work. We cannot disconnect from our source and expect our lives to work. It's that simple.

Reflect on Psalm 119:147–148. *"I rise before the dawning of the morning, and cry for help; I hope in Your word. My eyes are awake through the night watches that I may meditate on your word."*

Every day we have a multitude of chances to depend on Him. We need to train ourselves, for lack of a better way to put it, for a heightened ability to depend on Him. This is only possible if we are willing do something first—surrender. Yes, we talked about this already, but it is always in play. Many of us have given up our lives and hearts in general to Him; we have been saved. From there we can give over (surrender) our jobs, spouses, children, desires, dreams, places we live, ways we serve, and so on. The deeper our surrender, the deeper the relationship and the deeper the protection. We need to remember this! We need a daily refreshing of our hearts' and minds' surrender, the choice to say, "I am yours—use me today." You see, friends, there are miracles are in the surrender because we let go of the outcome and this brings God much honor! Remember, we are talking about the details of life here, the details of your every day, when we can say, "Lord, what do I do?" or "How do I go about this?" or "Lord, direct me here." I am talking about asking Him whether you should turn left or right, literally. Who needs a GPS? Want to sharpen your discernment? Drive somewhere you don't know how to get to and ask God to lead the way.

What kinds of things can we actively do to seek His guidance? We know there are lots. Let's think outside the box a bit and change up or add some of the things we can do. We can pray, go to church, dig into the Bible, listen to Christian music, attend bible studies, talk to other people, sharpen discernment, or memorize scripture. Add to the list if you can; I am sure there are more ways we can actively seek God's guidance in our daily lives. The key is to do it! The challenge is to ask Him about as many things as you possibly can in your walk. When in doubt, ask for wisdom. There are times, especially in the middle of some chaos, that you need to start there with wisdom. He gives freely and generously to those who ask. (James1:5). What's amazing to me is the merciful and tender help

He offers. Romans 8:26 takes away the obstacles we put in our own way when it comes to asking Him for help. *"Likewise the Spirit also helps in our weaknesses. For we do not know what we should pray for as we ought, but the Spirit Himself makes intercessions for us with groanings which cannot be uttered."* Wow!

For those of you who are busy, like me, finding ways to engage in the Word can sometimes prove to be a challenge. Getting creative with God is fun. When my children were small, we were in the car a lot. Having four children within five years, with a set of twins in there, really makes for a busy home. My ability to put on great worship music in the car was a game changer for me. Those songs were my prayers, and I let that music infuse my soul. God really does meet us where we are! Adding audio books to your time in the car or on the train is another great idea. Recently I discovered podcasts as well (yes, a little late!). These simple things could be just the answer; there are so many great ones out there.

We've talked about *how* to seek God's guidance. Let's explore *what* we should seek guidance for. Again, we are talking about the details of our lives, our daily lives. I am going to suggest that we aim to seek his guidance for everything. Some of you just fell off your chairs reading that—but yes, I meant *everything*. Our schedules, our tasks, our problems, our health, our relationships, finding our way out of traffic, where and how we should serve, where to sit in church, and so on. These details, and a million more, can be sought in Him. And why not? Why should we stick with the status quo? Why should we think we have it all figured out? Let's get off autopilot and engage with our Creator in a detail-based relationship. What I am suggesting is that we add one or two or five tomorrow and see how it goes. Just seek *more*. He loves it when we depend on Him. Surrendering our simple (and not-so-simple) daily tasks is a really easy way to deepen our relationship with Him. A huge benefit of a deeper relationship with God is more protection. If you don't think you need it, you're wrong. And if you don't think it's true, I dare you. We need more protection than we know. In 1 Peter

5:8, it says, *"Be self-controlled and alert, your enemy the devil prowls around like a roaring lion looking for someone to devour."* Anything we can surrender to God in our daily tasks and depend on Him for makes us more alert, because it removes us from automatic pilot. This simple act protects us and our families more than if we had just gone about our regular days. And it's more fun! I love seeing where He is going to take me or what He may ask me to do. We simply must be open and alert.

Perhaps there is a thorn in your side that you would love to get rid of? Give it over and ask Him to handle it. Be willing to be obedient to what He may ask. As we know, He may have you keep it. The Apostle Paul's life shows us that sometimes He can work a greater good in us if we keep the thorn. I know, without a doubt, that the God who knows us best knows how to keep us close to Him; thorns will do just that.

Give God more of your day and commit to following only His voice. I am in awe when I am in tune with Him. Doing our own thing on automatic pilot brings mediocrity and boredom, I find. Fall in love with His Word and His ways, and you just might find yourself on the best ride of your life!

There are many motivations for depending on God. Here are a few straight from Scripture.

Matthew 24:35
Heaven and earth will pass away, but My words will by no means pass away.

Isaiah 48:17
Thus says the Lord, your Redeemer, The Holy One of Israel: "I am the Lord, your God, Who teaches you to profit, Who leads you by the way you should go."

Psalm 119:105
Your word is a lamp to my feet, And a light to my path.

Psalm 143:10
Teach me to do Your will, For You are my God, Your Spirit is good, Lead me in the land of uprightness.

Psalm 145:17
The Lord is righteous in all His ways, Gracious in all His works.

We spoke earlier about being able to count on God because of His character. These scriptures reiterate that same thinking and further sum up why we can and should count on Him. He is a righteous and gracious teacher, who has our best outcomes at heart. I am a lover of people, but honestly, I don't know anyone who can be counted on like this—and add to that unfailingly, unceasingly, and without grievance. Wow, what a wonderful father!

Looking back for a moment, let's sum it up. We are to take who God is and our identity in Him and basically say, "Lead the way." We are to walk forward, depending on Him, based on His character and (the next section) His promises. Easy, right? Of course! The enemy plays a role in this by introducing doubt in any way, any place, and any time he can. Be onto it, and don't let up. Don't give in or back down. Stand firm on what you know! God is good, faithful, and larger than any doubt, fear, or obstacle.

CHAPTER 7

Promises of God

WE HAVE BY NOW ESTABLISHED THAT WE CAN COUNT on God and the reasons we should. The next beautiful segment, then, would look at what He says He can and will do for us. We've worked on a list (either mental or written or both) of what we can and do depend on Him for. That's *our* perspective; now let's look from *His* perspective. This will allow us to see our lists as a mere start to what we really have access to. Prepare to be blown away! As I wrote this section, it grew and grew the more I read about God and His names and His promises. I was overcome with complete and total awe. This section is by no means exhaustive, either. It's simply a solid start.

The breakthrough idea here is that God's plan for my life is far better than anything I could ever plan for myself. Jeremiah 29:11–14 says, *"'For I know the plans I have for you,' declares the Lord, 'plans to prosper you and not to harm you, plans to give you hope and a future. Then you will call on me and come and pray to me, and I will listen to you. You will seek me and find me when you seek me with all your heart. I will be found by you,' declares the Lord, 'and will bring you back from captivity. I will gather you from all the nations and places where I have banished you,' declares the Lord, 'and will bring you back to the place from which I carried you into exile."* I have personally stood on this over and over. Life is made up of a whole lot of days strung together that we live out. We need to be tied to his purposes *daily* so that we can be used to fully serve Him. Still, though, we need to believe that His plans for us are better than our plans for ourselves. This is, unfortunately, where many of us fall short. This is about trust. For those of us who came from a place in life where people didn't always have our backs, this concept might be a bit of a stretch—I get that, really. So now, there is a choice to make, right? Faced with this scripture, which is truth, the question is do we allow it to be *our* truth? I did. Please do too.

When we trust God, this is what we can expect to happen, according to Jeremiah 17:7–8: *"Blessed is the man who trusts in the Lord and whose hope is in the Lord. For he shall be like a tree planted by the waters, which spreads out its roots by the river, and will not fear when heat comes; but its leaf will be green and will not be anxious in the year of drought, nor will cease from yielding fruit."*

Standing on some of these scriptures also brings up another wonderful thing to depend on God for: His *promises*. In my growth as a Christian over almost two decades, I am continuing to learn many of His promises. I have had the opportunity to live out some of the promises He spoke over me personally, and some I have stood on from Scripture. What's so wonderful is that God's Word doesn't change. He doesn't lie; when He says something, it's a done deal. Whether the promise is from His Word or it's a personal promise concerning your life, it will come to pass. Active faith, surrender, daily talk (prayer), and yearning in your heart for Him will help His blessings become real.

Remember, promises allows us to stand on what we know about the character of God, about how He cherishes us all. We can use these to increase our faith or, better yet, know where to place it. God's Word is all-truthful and alive, and so His character in and of itself is a promise. Psalm 119:160 expresses this. *"The entirety of Your word is truth, and every one of Your righteous judgements endures forever."* The fact that He is consistent is a promise. That He saves is a promise. That He heals is a promise. That His purposes for our lives are good and hopeful are promises. That we are daughters and sons of the King, princes and princesses, His heirs, is a beautiful promise. That he gives us beauty for ashes is a promise. We can hold all of these near and dear to our hearts—promise!

God gives us the Promise of Provision

God's Word is full of promises to provide. When it comes to provision, I want to be clear that I am not specifically talking about money. In fact, I am really, actually, emphatically *not* talking about money. What I *am* talking about, is the desire and ability of God to provide for us what we need when we need it. From His perspective that may or may not include money, but I will leave that to Him to decide.

I have said before that God meets us where we are at. When it comes to provision, this couldn't be truer. God brings us comfort when we need it. He uses people and their words and their actions (like hugs) at moments when we need them. Don't underestimate the stranger who asks you, "Are you okay?" God gives us His Grace the moment we need grace. He gives us mercy the moment we need mercy. He gives us patience when we need patience. He gives us clarity when we need it. He gives us gentleness when we need that, too. There is nothing He cannot do. There is no problem that is too big, no circumstance that He can't handle. *"Ah, Lord God! Behold, You have made the heavens and the earth by Your great power and outstretched arm, there is nothing too hard for you."* Jeremiah 32:17 Provision is His business!

There is no end to the things He can provide us when we need them. Now don't get me wrong here—things don't fall out of the sky. The point is, the surrendered believer is in position to ask. In fact, the surrendered believer is in position to come boldly to the throne. In Hebrews 4:16, it says, *"Let us therefore come boldly to the throne of grace, that we may obtain mercy and find grace to help in time of need."* We must acknowledge that we are not puppets. We need to be open to receiving help and, of course, recognize it when it shows up! We need to ask and invite Him into the exact situation and moments in which we are struggling. And here is the cool thing; what He gives us is not the strength to be those things in our weakened ability right then, but He gives us His strength, from Him, so that we may rest in Him. God gives us from His very own heart and personality the things we need. He offers us that which belongs to Him. His grace. His mercy. His gentleness. His wisdom. His perspective. His love. The provision is genuinely Him, in the exact form we need it. I would much rather enjoy the blessing of the provision He is willing to give than to strive in my inability to be or have those things that I need and perhaps fail miserably. This is depending on God for the fine details.

Our depending on Him like this through the most intimate details of our days means He gets all the glory. We need be careful of thinking we have it all under control. We should revel in the times when we don't, so we can invite our good and gracious God to show up and be present. The Apostle Peter says it like this, from 2 Peter: 3–4: *"As His divine power has given to us all things that pertain to life and godliness, through the knowledge of Him who called us by glory and virtue, by which have been given to us exceedingly great and precious promises, that through these you may be partakers of the divine nature, having escaped the corruption that is in the world through lust."* Divine nature, you say? Why yes, that is exactly what we get. We get to be a part of His beautiful divine Self as He shares Himself with us!

Let's expand on some of these and add a few more.

God Gives Us the Provision of Himself

As God:

Psalm 73:26
My flesh and heart fail: but God is the strength of my heart and my portion forever.

Joshua 1:9
Have I not commanded you? Be strong and of good courage; do not be afraid, nor be dismayed, for the Lord your God is with you wherever you go.

Psalm 121:2
My help comes from the Lord, the Maker of heaven and earth.

And I absolutely love this one:

Isaiah 41:10
Fear not, for I am with you; Be not dismayed, for I am your God. I will strengthen you, yes, I will uphold you with My righteous right hand.

As Jesus:

John 14:6
I am the way, the truth, and the life. No one comes to the Father except through Me.

1 John 5:12
Whoever has the Son has life; whoever does not have the Son of God does not have life.

As the Holy Spirit: The Holy Spirit, available to all who believe, was given as a beautiful gift. There are some amazing benefits of having the Holy Spirit reside in us. If we look at the names and references, we see He is the Comforter, Helper, Teacher, and Guide.

Luke 11:13
If you then, though you are evil, know how to give good gifts to your children, how much more will your Father in heaven give the Holy Spirit to those who ask Him!

John 14:16–17
And I will pray to the Father, and He will give you another Helper, that He may abide with you forever—the Spirit of truth, whom the world cannot receive, because it neither sees Him nor knows Him; but you know Him, for He dwells with you and will be in you.

John 14:26
But the Advocate, the Holy Spirit, whom the Father will send in my name, will teach you all things and will remind you of everything I have said to you.

Acts 1:3–5
After his suffering, he presented himself to them and gave many convincing proofs that he was alive. He appeared to them over a period of forty days and spoke about the kingdom of God. On one occasion, while he was eating with them, he gave them this command: "Do not leave Jerusalem, but wait for the gift my Father promised, which you have heard me speak about. For John baptized with water, but in a few days, you will be baptized with the Holy Spirit."

Ephesians 1:12–14
In order that we, who were the first to put our hope in Christ, might be for the praise of his glory. And you also were included in Christ when you heard the message of truth, the gospel of your salvation. When you believed, you were marked in him with a seal, the promised Holy Spirit, who is a deposit guaranteeing our inheritance until the redemption of those who are God's possession—to the praise of his glory.

God Gives Us the Provision of His Word

Psalm 119:160
The entirety of Your word is truth, and every one of Your righteous judgements endures forever.

Matthew 4:4
But He answered and said, "It is written, Man shall not live by bread alone, but by every word that proceeds from the mouth of God."

Psalm 119:140
Your promises have been thoroughly tested, and your servant loves them.

Psalm 18:30
As for God, His way is perfect: The Lord's word is flawless; he shields all who take refuge in Him.

Hebrews 4:12
For the word of God is living and powerful, and sharper than any two-edged sword, piercing even to the division of soul and spirit, and of joints and marrow, and is a discerner of the thoughts and intents of the heart.

God Gives Us the Provision of Protection

Psalm 119:114
You are my hiding place and my shield, I hope in Your word.

Psalm 121:3
He will not let your foot slip, he who watches over you will not slumber.

Psalm 31:4
Keep me free from the trap that is set for me, for you are my refuge.

Psalm 40:11
Do not withhold Your tender mercies from me, O Lord; let Your lovingkindness and Your truth continually preserve me.

Psalm 18:30
As for God, His way is perfect; the word of the Lord is proven; He is a shield to all who trust in Him.

Isaiah 41:10
So do not fear, for I am with you; do not be dismayed, for I am your God. I will strengthen you and help you; I will uphold you with my righteous right hand.

Isaiah 41:13
For I am the Lord your God who takes hold of your right hand and says to you, "Do not fear; I will help you."

Psalm 27:1
The Lord is my light and my salvation—whom shall I fear? The Lord is the stronghold of my life—of whom shall I be afraid?

Nahum 1:7
The Lord is good, a stronghold in the day of trouble; and He knows those who trust Him.

Romans 8:28
And we know that all things work together for good to those who love God and are called according to His purposes.

Romans 8:31
What then shall we say to these things? If God is for us, who can be against us?

Ephesians 6:10–13
Finally, my brethren, be strong in the Lord and in the power of His might. Put on the whole armor of God, that you may be able to stand against the wiles of the devil. For we do not wrestle against flesh and blood, but against principalities, against powers, against the rulers of the darkness of this age, against spiritual hosts of wickedness in the heavenly places. Therefore, take up the whole armor of God, that you may be able to withstand in the evil day, having done all, to stand.

God Gives Us the Provision of Wisdom

Psalm 119:144
Your statutes are always righteous; give me understanding that I may live.

Proverbs 2:1–6, 10–11
My son, if you receive my words, and treasure my commands within you, so that you incline your ear to wisdom, and apply your heart to understanding; yes, if you cry out for discernment, and lift up your voice for understanding, if you seek her as silver, and search for her as for hidden treasures, then you will understand the fear of the Lord, and find the knowledge of God. For the Lord gives wisdom; from His mouth come knowledge and understanding; He stores up sound wisdom for the upright … When wisdom enters your heart, and knowledge is pleasant to your soul, discretion will preserve you; understanding will keep you.

James 1:5
If any of you lacks wisdom, you should ask God, who gives generously to all without finding fault, and it will be given to you.

God Gives Us the Provision of Grace

Psalm 84:11
For the Lord God is a sun and a shield; the Lord will give grace and glory; no good thing will He withhold from those who walk uprightly.

Proverbs 3:34
Surely, He scorns the scornful, but gives grace to the humble.

Romans 1:5
Through Him we have received grace and apostleship for obedience to the faith among all nations for His name.

2 Corinthians 12:9
But he said to me, "My grace is sufficient for you, for my power is made perfect in weakness. Therefore, I will boast all the more gladly about my weaknesses, so that Christ's power may rest on me."

1 Timothy 1:14
And the grace of our Lord was exceedingly abundant, with faith and love which are in Christ Jesus.

Grace also administers peace. Because grace is from God, we get a part of Him, which brings peace. Be open to grace. Recognize it. Revel in it.

God Gives Us the Provision of Deliverance

Isaiah 46:3–4
Listen to me, you descendants of Jacob, all the remnant of the people of Israel, you whom I have upheld since your birth, and have carried since you were born. Even to your old age and gray hairs, I am he, I am he who will sustain you. I have made you and will carry you, I will sustain you and I will rescue you.

That scripture shows us God's intention to deliver us. He is constantly on our side and wants to help us stay free from sin and the strongholds it creates.

Exodus 14:13
Moses answered the people, "Do not be afraid. Stand firm and you will see the deliverance the Lord will bring you today. The Egyptians you see today you will never see again. The Lord will fight for you; you need only to be still."

Psalm 40:17
But I am poor and needy; yet the Lord thinks upon me. You are my help and my deliverer; do not delay, O my God.

Daniel 3:17
If we are thrown into the blazing furnace, the God we serve is able to deliver us from it, and he will deliver us from your Majesty's hand.

Sometimes we need to be delivered, not just from the sin we enslave ourselves in but from the plots of evil and schemes of the enemy. God is able to do this. Like Daniel, we need be aware (as we have discussed previously) and confess the strength and dependence of our God. When we speak out loud, we put action to our beliefs and faith, and all the powers of our magnificent Father can go to work! This scripture shows our part in the process and the action of being delivered.

Romans 8:38–39
For I am persuaded that neither death nor life, nor angels nor principalities nor powers, not things present nor things to come, nor height nor depth, nor any other created thing, shall be able to separate us from the love of God which is in Christ Jesus our Lord.

1 Peter 2:9
But you are a chosen generation, a royal priesthood, a holy nation, His own special people, that you may proclaim the praises of Him who called you out of darkness into His marvelous light.

There is the reference to "end times" deliverance, also found here:

Daniel 12:1
At that time Michael, the great prince who protects your people, will arise. There will be a time of distress such as has not happened from the beginning of nations until then. But at that time your people—everyone whose name is found written in the book—will be delivered.

Jesus in Jeans

When we are deep in the ditches of despair, discouragement, and sin, Jesus comes along and takes note. He loves us so much that He takes off His white robe, puts on His jeans, and climbs in with us, all the way to the bottom. He has already been there, on the cross and in the tomb. But He was victorious over death and the grave. The Deliverer offers deliverance to us; we need only accept it. He is the Help, the Saviour, the Answer. He lifts us out with His mercy and grace. He does for us what we cannot do for ourselves. Hallelujah!

God gives us Personal Promises

Genesis 28:15
I am with you and will watch over you wherever you go, and I will bring you back to this land. I will not leave you until I have done what I have promised you.

Romans 8:37
Yet in all these things we are more than conquerors through Him who loved us.

2 Corinthians 6:16–18
What agreement is there between the temple of God and idols? For we are the temple of the living God. As God has said: "I will live with them and walk among them, and I will be their God, and they will be my people. Therefore, come out from them and be separate," says the Lord. "Touch no unclean thing, and I will receive you. And I will be a Father to you and you will be my sons and daughters," says the Lord Almighty."

Seeking God's personal promises and having Him walk alongside us is one of the most important key actions and states of heart we can aspire to. His personal Word over each of our lives could seriously be the *actual thing* that gets us through. Honestly speaking, the last twenty-four months has seen this proven true in my life. God's Word over me and my family has freed me, consoled me, strengthened me, and enabled me to persevere when I couldn't see it was possible. Friends, I plead with you to seek truth. Seek it, find it, embrace it, and walk out what it is He wants from you. He promises not to leave you. He promises to walk it with you and to work it out with you—not *for* you. Are you willing to do the same?

I can't tell you how many times I was desperate for God to show me what to do in certain situations. I would open my Bible and look for His words, His comfort, and His promises. And He never failed to provide. Yet sometimes there are situations that need a more personal approach. I am talking about the approach that pours forth your heart-wrenching issues to Jesus, lands them at the foot of the cross, and begs, "Now what?"

God Promises Us an Intimate Relationship

2 Corinthians 6:16–18
And what agreement has the temple of God with idols? For you are the temple of the living God. As God has said: "I will dwell in them and walk among them. I will be their God, and they shall be my people." Therefore, "Come out from among them and be separate," says the Lord. "Do not touch what is unclean, And I will receive you. I will be a Father to you, and you shall be My sons and daughters," says the Lord Almighty.

Romans 8:35, 37–39
Who shall separate us from the love of Christ? Shall tribulation, or distress, or persecution, or famine, or nakedness, or peril, or sword? Yet in all these things we are more than conquerors through Him who loved us. For I am persuaded that neither death nor life, nor angels nor principalities nor powers, nor things present nor things to come, nor height nor depth, nor

any other created thing, shall be able to separate us from the love of God, which is in Christ Jesus our Lord.

Isaiah 46:4
Even to your old age, I am He, and even to gray hairs I will carry you! I have made, and I will bear; even I will carry, and will deliver you.

Psalm 25:14
The secret of the Lord is with those who fear Him, and He will show them His covenant.

Philippians 1:6
Being confident of this very thing, that He who has begun a good work in you will complete it until the day of Jesus Christ.

God Promises Us Personal Gifts

Acts 10:44–46
While Peter was still speaking these words, the Holy Spirit fell upon all those who heard the word. And those of the circumcision who believed were astonished, as many as came with Peter, because the gift of the Holy Spirit had been poured out on the Gentiles also, For they heard them speak with tongues and magnify God.

Romans 12:3, 6–8
For I say, through the grace given to me, to everyone who is among you, not to think of himself more highly than he ought to think, but to think soberly, as God has dealt to each one a measure of faith ... Having then gifts differing according to the grace that is given to us, let us use them; if prophecy, let us prophesy in proportion to our faith; or ministry, let us use it in our ministering; he who teaches, in teaching; he who exhorts, in exhortation; he who gives, with liberality; he who leads, with diligence; he who shows mercy, with cheerfulness.

2 Timothy 1:7
For God has not given us a spirit of fear, but of power and of love and a sound mind.

Don't let the enemy tell you otherwise!

1 Corinthians 7:17
But as God has distributed to each one, as the Lord has called to each one, so let him walk.

1 Corinthians 12:1–11
Now concerning spiritual gifts, brethren, I do not want you to be ignorant; You know that you were Gentiles, carried away to these dumb idols, however you were led. Therefore, I make known to you that no one speaking by the Spirit of God calls Jesus accursed, and no one can say that Jesus is Lord except by the Holy Spirit. There are diversities of gifts, but the same Spirit. There are differences of ministries, but the same Lord. And there are diversities of activities, but it is the same God who works all in all. But the manifestation of the Spirit is given to each one for the profit of all; for to one is given the word of wisdom through the Spirit, to another the word of knowledge through the same Spirit, to another faith by the same Spirit, to another gifts of healings by the same Spirit, to another the working of miracles, to another prophecy, to another discerning of spirits, to another different kinds of tongues, to another the interpretation of tongues. But one and the same Spirit works all these things, distributing to each one individually as He wills.

I think this is as good as spot as any to take a minute and talk about comparison. "Comparison?" you ask. Stay with me here. We must discuss this, because the enemy has set a trap for all of us, called comparison, and we need to address it. Comparison is a true stealer of joy!

Everyone wants to fit in. Everybody needs to know how they fit into their world. It's just natural to wonder and ponder. Our role in the universe is worth discovering. When we aren't aware of our identity in Christ, though, we sometimes try to find it by comparing ourselves to others, to see how we measure up. This is not usually pretty. I call it a trap because it's based on lies. The scriptures above point out how God has made us each with different gifts and different callings. Provided we believe these things, we have a fighting chance. But the enemy wants us to believe that our lives compared to others' aren't worth much and that we are inferior to them. Who is "them"? It can be pretty much anyone we see. This comparison isn't confined to our own personal spheres, either—it's worldwide. Growing up before the internet and cell phones, my sphere of comparison (as an unsaved teenager) was as far as my eyes could see, and that was it, with perhaps the odd magazine cover included. Nowadays our children (and we, too) are subjected to the onslaught of social media and unrealistic portrayals of other people's lives. As long as we look out and not in, we suffer the temptation to think that what we have just isn't good enough. So we buy that car or that house or go on a certain vacation; we buy that Prada bag, lose twenty pounds, change our hair and makeup, et cetera—and then what? The next week we find something else we are "missing." This is exactly why Jesus said, *"But seek first the kingdom of God and His righteousness, and all these things shall be added to you."* (Matthew 6:33)

Comparison works in two ways. It either makes you feel inferior to others, or it creates self-righteousness, making you feel better about yourself but at the other person's expense. Either way, it steals your joy and energy. It distracts you from finding out who you really are by suggesting that you should be just like someone else. Your life is yours, your race is yours, and your identity is yours—why be like someone else? It simply won't work.

God Promises Us Hope

Romans 15:13
Now may the God of hope fill you with all joy and peace in believing; that you may abound in hope by the power of the Holy Spirit.

1 Peter 1:3–4
Blessed be the God and Father of our Lord Jesus Christ, who according to his abundant mercy has begotten us again to a living hope through the resurrection of Jesus Christ from the dead, to an inheritance incorruptible and undefiled and that does not fade away, reserved in heaven for you.

Ultimately, Jesus's vacant tomb tells us that what He did for Himself He can, and surely will, do for us. There is hope in knowing that nothing is too hard for Him to work in us and our lives. It may look dark now, but there is always a resurrection!

Romans 5:1–5
Therefore, having been justified by faith, we have peace with God through our Lord Jesus Christ, through whom also we have access by faith into this grace in which we stand, and rejoice in hope of the glory of God. And not only that, but we also glory in tribulations, knowing that tribulation produces perseverance; and perseverance, character; and character, hope. Now hope does not disappoint, because the love of God has been poured out in our hearts by the Holy Spirit who was given to us.

Romans 15:13
Now may the God of hope fill you with all joy and peace in believing, that you may abound in hope by the power of the Holy Spirit.

I love those verses from Romans, and they make a perfect transition and addition to the next topic, that of sanctification.

God Promises Us Sanctification

God desires His children be "set apart" from the world. We should talk differently, walk differently, think differently, and love differently than those who don't know Him—right? He desires to make us holy and refined so that we bear His image. This process is lifelong, and He promises to never stop working *in* us that which He wishes to work *out* in us. Philippians 1:6 says *He who has begun a good work in you will complete it until the day of Jesus Christ.* God will never stop helping us be more like him; that process is sanctification.

Paul describes this very concept and gives direction to his readers on how to behave like Christians. Please note that some of this may hurt!

Romans 12:9–21
Let love be without hypocrisy. Abhor what is evil. Cling to what is good. Be kindly affectionate to one another with brotherly love, in honor giving preference to one another, not lagging in diligence, fervent in spirit, serving the Lord; rejoicing in hope, patient in tribulation, continuing steadfastly in prayer, distributing to the needs of the saints, given to hospitality. Bless those who persecute you; bless and do not curse. Rejoice with those who rejoice, and weep with those who weep. Be of the same mind toward one another. Do not set your mind on high things, but associate with the humble. Do not be wise in your own opinion. Repay no one evil for evil. Have regard for good things in the sight of all men. If it is possible, as much as depends on you, live peaceably with all men. Beloved, do not avenge yourselves, but rather give place to wrath; for it is written, "Vengeance is Mine, I will repay, says the Lord." Therefore, "If your enemy is hungry, feed him; if he is thirsty, give him a drink; for in doing so you will heap coals of fire on his head." Do not be overcome by evil, but overcome evil with good.

Tall order? Yes, so book done, and we can all get on our way with that, right? It is so important to know, without a doubt, that if someone whom we have been around for a while found out that we were Christians, it would make sense to them. It's imperative that our outer walk matches our inner one and that it can be seen.

Ultimately, here is the truth about working it out:

Zechariah 13:9
I will bring the one-third through the fire, will refine them as silver is refined, and test them as gold is tested. They will call on My name, and I will answer them. I will say "This is my people"; and each one will say "The Lord is my God."

Psalm 66:10
For you, O God, have tested us; You have refined us as silver is refined.

Jesus says it like this, as written by John:

John 17:17
Sanctify them by your truth. Your word is truth.

The Word of God is described by Paul in a way that helps to expand this:

Hebrews 4:12
For the word of God is living and powerful, and sharper than any two-edged sword, piercing even to the division of soul and spirit, and of joints and marrow, and is a discerner of the thoughts and intent of the heart.

If we are willing to infuse our hearts, souls, and minds with the Word of God, we will find a guide like no other. The Word changes our hearts, renews our thoughts, lifts our spirits, and grounds our actions more distinctively than anything we have experienced. I know many lovely Christians who are not familiar with the Word of God outside church. Some of them don't even own a bible or open the one they have, and they struggle with conviction, joy, and peace. Well, it's no wonder! The "living" word of God offers us the direction and authentication we so desperately seek elsewhere. We must use it to cut to the core of our problems and let it help us find our contentment and peace. We must allow it to remind us we're not alone, in strife or praise. Read it. Listen to it. Love it.

God Promises Us a Royal Identity

2 Corinthians 5:17
Therefore, if anyone is in Christ, he is a new creation; old things have passed away; behold, all things have become new.

I spoke of this at length earlier, but it needs to be repeated! Our discussion in the previous chapter was about our identity in Christ, not in circumstances or experiences of the world. When we have our identities in Him, we have royal identities. I love this verse as well because of the word *behold*, which indicates "to see with attention and observe with care." No more status quo. No more mediocrity. This new creation is a thing of beauty and wonder and should be taken note of. It is no small detail, this royal identity we inherit when we join the Body of Christ!

Romans 8:16–17
The Spirit Himself bears witness with our spirit that we are children of God, and if children, then heirs—heirs of God and joint heirs with Christ, if indeed we suffer with Him, that we may also be glorified together.

Galatians 3:26, 29
For you are all sons of God through faith in Jesus Christ ... and if you are Christ's, then you are Abraham's seed, and heirs according to the promise.

Ephesians 3:6
That the Gentiles should be fellow heirs, of the same body, and partakers of His promise in Christ through the gospel.

Titus 3:7
That having been justified by His grace we should become heirs according to the hope of eternal life.

Finally comes this one, which I love:

James 2:5
Listen, my beloved brethren: Has God not chosen the poor of this world to be rich in faith and heirs of the kingdom, which He promised to those who love Him?

Don't ever let anyone try to tell you that you are not royalty. You absolutely are!

God Promises Us the Gift of Mercy

I have recently been suffering from migraine headaches. These are very different from regular headaches and can affect your daily life dramatically. If you have never had a migraine, then this may seem silly to state, but please read on. If you have had migraine headaches, then you already know the pain, and the memory of your last one probably popped into mind. In your heart you may even feel sorry for me because you know the anguish they can cause. As I described my last bout, which had me in bed for four days, to a friend who also suffered, she said, "Honey, I know exactly how you feel. Let me know what I can do." The empathy in her eyes melted me. The tone of her voice comforted me. It was very different from the comfort that others who didn't understand could give.

We all long for people to understand us and our circumstances, to know how we feel and then to act on it, if necessary. Not everyone can do this, and it can be very frustrating. Fortunately, we serve a God who was like us in every way but sin. He can give us the mercy we ache for, because He truly understands all things, and like my friend who suffered migraines as well, He has also suffered. He is willing to give us the mercy that cleanses our souls, wipes our slates clean of sin, and heals our broken hearts. Let Him. Some of us have been stuck in a pit of guilt or pride (traps of the enemy) or some other thing that keeps us from believing that we're worthy of His mercy. Our Jesus in Jeans helps us climb up out of the pit and allows mercy to flow to us and through us. By mercy and grace, we have salvation. It is by mercy and grace that any time after that we can start fresh. The pit of sin need not keep us from what we ache for.

Regarding mercy, it goes like this: You can generally only give as much as you have received. We have the opportunity to freely pass on the mercy we have been given. I'm not referring to the mercy that someone tried to give us, but the mercy we have allowed ourselves to receive when it was extended to us. The mercy of God is a never-ending, always-full-to-the-brim-and-ready-to-pour-out-on-you kind of mercy. Allowing ourselves the gift of receiving it is key. We can totally depend on Him to have it, but we must be connected enough to allow Him to give it.

John 3:16–17
For God so loved the world that He gave His only begotten Son, that whoever believes in Him should not perish but have everlasting life. For God did not send His Son into the world to condemn the world, but that the world through Him might be saved.

God's giving Jesus to us is the ultimate act of mercy. Jesus became one of us to be the bridge between this life and the next. Because of God's unfathomable mercy, we have access to heaven and heaven here on earth.

Deuteronomy 7:9
Therefore know that the Lord your God, he is God, the faithful God who keeps covenant and mercy for a thousand generations with those who love Him and keep His commandments.

1 Chronicles 16:34
Oh, give thanks to the Lord, for He is good! His mercy endures forever.

Psalm 5:7
But as for me, I will come into Your house in the multitude of Your mercy; in fear of You I will worship toward your holy temple.

Psalm 23:6
Surely goodness and mercy shall follow me all the days of my life; and I will dwell in the house of the Lord forever.

Psalm 86:5
For You, Lord, are good, and ready to forgive, and abundant in mercy to all those who call upon You.

Psalm 86:13, 15
For great is Your mercy toward me, and You have delivered my soul from the depths of Sheol ... But You, O Lord, are a God full of compassion, and gracious, longsuffering and abundant in mercy and truth.

Psalm 100:5
For the Lord is good; His mercy is everlasting, and all His truth endures to all generations.

Psalm 103:8, 10–12
The Lord is merciful and gracious, slow to anger, and abounding in mercy ... He has not dealt with us according to our sins, nor punished us according to our iniquities. For as the heavens are high above the earth, so great is His mercy toward those who fear him; as far as the east is from the west, so far has He removed our transgressions from us.

Psalm 136 repeats twenty-six times *"For His mercy endures forever."* He is truly merciful. He was never more merciful than when He saved us by hanging on a cross. He is continually merciful as He saves us and provides for us. We simply don't deserve it.

Luke 1:50
And His mercy is on those who fear Him from generation to generation.

Romans 9:15–16
For He says to Moses, "I will have mercy on whomever I will have mercy, and I will have compassion on whomever I will have compassion." So, then it is not of him who wills, nor of him who runs, but of God who shows mercy.

Ephesians 2:4–7
But God, who is rich in mercy, because of His great love with which He loved us, even when we were dead in trespasses, made us alive together with Christ (by grace you have been saved), and raised us up together, and made us sit together in the heavenly places in Christ Jesus, that in the ages to come He might show us the exceeding riches of His grace in His kindness toward us in Christ Jesus.

Not only does mercy exemplify His character, but it is motivation for His actions. After writing this section and reading through these amazing verses, I want to fall on the floor in worship. I have been so struck by the love and by the character of God that it has made me stop typing. My heart has filled with awe and my eyes with tears as the overwhelming feeling of pure compassion flows over me. I have chosen to reference so many scriptures because mercy is, in my opinion, something most people have lived without to a large degree. Believing in the mercy of God allows us to feel His love in our hearts and count on Him to take tender care of our souls. Mercy is also so close to forgiveness that it is hard to separate them. God's mercy on us motivated Him to give us Jesus, the ultimate avenue of forgiveness. We have it once and for all *and* ongoing. It truly is unfathomable. So please, don't try to make sense of it—just go with it! Abounding and unending mercy is yours and mine. Hallelujah!

God Promises Us We Will Be Heard

A concept very closely related to depending on God for guidance is this very important one, the concept that He truly *hears* us. This idea may seem trivial, but I want to leave no stone unturned. It is imperative that we grasp this, because it is integral to our relationship with Him, and to our victory. How many of us have someone in our lives whom we talk to, but they just don't listen? Or they listen but they really don't hear us? Jeremiah 29:12 has the Lord saying, *"Then you will call upon me and go and pray to me, and I will listen to you."* He says, *"I will"*! So, it was a done deal, one hundred per cent. He said it, so we need to believe that He hears us: our silent prayers, our out-loud prayers, our talk-out-loud-as-if-he-is-right-next-to-us prayers. If we can't believe he hears us, then pouring out our hearts is futile. We might as well close this book up right now. We need to trust that he does. He wants our prayers. He wants our heartbreak and fears and thoughts and questions. He wants it all. Some of you, like me, grew up just wanting to be heard. I absolutely know now and count on the fact that God hears me.

Matthew 11:28–29
Come to me, all you who labor and are heavy laden, and I will give you rest. Take my yoke upon you and learn from me, for I am gentle and lowly in heart, and you will find rest for your souls.

There are some things only He can hear, only he can bear, only he can mend. Know this. Count on this. Depend on this.

Psalm 118:5–6
I called on the Lord in distress; The Lord answered me and set me in a broad place. The Lord is on my side; I will not fear. What can man do to me?

Psalm 145:18–19
The Lord is near to all those who call upon Him, to all who call upon Him in truth. He will fulfill the desire of those who fear Him. He also will hear their cry and save them.

Psalm 120:1
In my distress I cried to the Lord, and He heard me.

Psalm 116:1–2
I love the Lord, because He has heard my voice and my supplications. Because He has inclined His ear to me, therefore I will call upon him as long as I live.

Jeremiah 33:3
Call to me, and I will answer you, and tell you great and unsearchable things you do not know.

1 John 5:14–15
Now this is the confidence that we have in Him. That if we ask anything according to His will, He hears us. And if we know that He hears us, whatever we ask, we know that we have the petition that we have asked Him.

Did you ever talk to someone who was nodding and saying "mm-hmm" every once in a while, but you knew they were not listening at all? Or have you talked to someone whose version of listening is waiting for her turn to talk? Every day, right? Talking to God is so different. He really hears. He really listens. The best part is that He knows *exactly* what you need. Yay, God! The question is, will you take the time to talk to him (prayer) and listen for answers (usually prayer)? I think it is safe to say that a sacrifice of time is essential on the road to victory.

Some of us have the talking to God aspect down, but we lack when it comes to listening. Unfortunately, many of us are listening to incessant chatter, either outwardly or inwardly. We have not figured out how to turn our brains off and be quiet; there is constant babble going on in our heads. Unfortunately, we can't hear God too well if this is the case. Is it any wonder that so many people believe God is not talking to them? The truth is, they are unavailable to hear what He has to say. Here are some suggestions to quiet your mind. Take lunch alone, get up early (my personal favourite), take a walk, go to listening prayer, and turn the radio or television off. I am sure there are more, but I think you get what I am saying. We just need to commit to some quiet time to let our tender God do His thing. He does have a lot to say. Digging into a bible is probably one of the most valuable things we can do when we want to know what God has to say. Take courage, sacrifice some time that might just be wasted anyway, and open your heart. I bet you will be amazed!

God Promises Us That the Maker of the Universe Is Our Daddy

As we close out this list of things we can count on God for, there is one more item I wish to cover. His relationship with us takes on many forms. Let's talk about turning the gem of his character to show the facet of daddy. The concept of God as Father, as in *my* father, was very unfamiliar to me until just a few years into my journey. Growing up without a father, I had no idea the impact allowing Him this role would have in my life. I grasped the I'm-a-princess part extremely quickly, but the other part took some time. I *am* a daughter, but I had not had the opportunity to *be* a daughter in my life. I do believe that a whole book can be written on just this one topic; the impact on our hearts and lives is so dynamic and so dramatic, and this one aspect can heal us in ways we didn't know even existed.

A relationship so intimate and caring, so gentle and fulfilling, is what God desires us to have with him. His will for us is that our hearts are safe and protected, that our dreams are shared, that our fears are known to Him, and that while He is the God who sees all, He is a Father who knows and loves us anyway. Many of the characteristics of God and His promises stem from this one thing, the fact that He really is our Daddy.

Romans 8:15
For you did not receive the spirit of bondage again to fear, but you received the Spirit of adoption by whom we cry out, "Abba, Father."

Galatians 4:3–7
This so beautifully explains it: *Even so we, when we were children, were in bondage under the elements of the world. But when the fullness of time had come, God sent forth His son, born of a woman, born under the law, to redeem those who were under the law, that we might receive adoption as sons. And because you are sons, God has sent forth the Spirit of His Son into your hearts, crying out, "Abba, Father!" Therefore you are no longer a slave but a son, and if a son, then an heir of God through Christ.*

The "Abba, Father" term denotes the close and intimate relationship fathers of the time had with their children and the trust their children had in them. To have an "Abba" relationship with God is so much deeper than being a child of God by reference. Surrendering is part of this equation, as it is in many of the other principles discussed earlier. Unfortunately, many people whose relationships with their earthly fathers were inferior have a hard time adapting to these truths. I don't know why it was easy for me. It just was. Lacking that earthly relationship made it a very uncomplicated issue. I pray that those of you with similar circumstances will allow His tender and merciful love to pour over you.

PRINCIPLES 2 AND 3: HUMILITY AND SERVING

CHAPTER 8

A Humble Heart

LOOKING BACK AT THE SCRIPTURES, THE SECOND AND third principles that emerge are humility and serving. These principles are similar to the question of the chicken and the egg—which one comes first, humility or serving? Does being humble allow us to serve (better), or does serving make us humble? Think of humility. It's not that the chosen scriptures specifically speak of it, but it's more the *attitude* of the people who came to Jesus. They threw themselves at His feet, knowing He truly was great and worthy. Those people totally understood this, and they came humbly to Him. Their requests were made as desperate pleas; they knew exactly who they were asking. They knew His identity, and it helped them know their own; this is where humility comes in. This is a perfect addition to the identity portion as well.

The definition of humility is "the state or quality of being humble." It is a disposition. It is the "freedom from pride and arrogance, a lowliness of mind, a sense of one's own unworthiness through imperfection and sinfulness." Essentially, humility allows us to recognize and acknowledge our connection to God. In this there is a letting go of self. Being aware of what we *are* is pride, and in pride there is an exaggeration of self, which also includes thinking that we can control things. The ability to depend on God daily and release or surrender ourselves to him, which we discussed earlier, helps build more humility into our characters, which is essential for our growth.

From what I have personally experienced, the more I depend on God, the humbler I become. Subsequently, the humbler I become, the more I *want* to depend on God. It's a beautiful thing!

Humility really becomes part of our new identities in Him. Paul, in his letter to the Colossians, spoke mostly of Christ at the centre of everything. He reminded the saved people in Colossae that nothing they did or knew was necessary or meant anything to their salvation. Jesus is it; nothing more is needed or can be added. After a short reprimand, he then talked about the "new man." This part of Scripture is a reminder that we *can* change, we *can* grow, and we *can* become more like Jesus. This very thing is a part of our walk; it is the walk, it is the goal, to be more like Jesus. *"If then you were raised with Christ, seek those things which are above, where Christ is, sitting at the right hand of God. Set your mind on things above, not on things of earth. For you died, and your life is hidden with Christ in God ... Therefore, as the elect of God, holy and beloved, put on tender mercies, kindness, meekness, longsuffering; bearing with one another, and forgiving one another, if anyone has a complaint against another; even as Christ forgave you, so you must do."* (Colossians 3:1–3, 12–13)

Our unworthiness of His love, affection, and forgiveness, once realized, presents a dependence on Christ the Healer, Christ the Saviour. We must truly come to terms with how much we don't deserve God's love before we can walk it out in a deep and meaningful way. When we understand this, humility is born. The goal is to keep it, to hold fast and long onto the reality that we can do nothing without Him and that He is our true and only source of life and victory. There is no way to even comprehend the magnitude of His love for us. We must simply give it up to faith. What follows is the realization that we can do nothing without him. *"I am the vine, you are the branches. He who abides in me and I in him, bears much fruit; for without Me you can do nothing."* (John 15:5) Total dependence is mandatory for victorious living. Yet an attitude of minimal faith prevents us from being totally dependent. Total dependence requires total humility.

In the famous Sermon on the Mount, Jesus spoke these words: "Blessed are the meek, for they shall inherit the earth." (Matthew 5:5). I speak of humility and meekness together; they are virtually interchangeable, with only a minor difference: meekness refers more to our conduct and humility more to our nature and opinions toward ourselves. In both, however, there is one constant, the absence of feeling that we are superior one to another. I believe God spoke of humility and meekness to give a contrast to his thoughts on pride. So, basically, he doubled up the teaching on pride, coming from both the presence and the absence of it.

There are a couple of misconceptions regarding humility that I would like to get out of the way here. One is the lie that low self-esteem is humility. Remember, our identities are in Him; therefore, we need not think lowly of ourselves. As He removes our sins and builds us up in Him, He removes the things that we throw our characters on. Stay with me here. As we release ourselves to Him (yes, that's the surrender we have been discussing) we will naturally grow in our esteem and think ourselves highly *in* Him. This cannot be confused with being proud and arrogant. Secondly, being meek and humble does not mean we are weak. "Meekness is not weakness" I recently read. Humility does not mean people have permission to take advantage of you. In this *me* society, the consensus goes against humility; it goes against vulnerability and openness to protect self. Self is ego. Ego is mind. Neither of these reflect spirit, and that is what we must actively protect. Humility is the way. In the community of Christ, we are called to be humble. God knows why.

Humility is meant to be a covering for us. Humility prevents us from being offended; it keeps our mouths closed at the appropriate times as well as opening the door to better listening, better relationships, service to others (and God), forgiveness, peace, and love. Humility is truly key in victorious living. God's heart is wide open to the humble heart! His blessings are all over the humble life.

Let's add some substantiating scriptures to finish this concept.

Zephaniah 2:3
Seek the Lord, all you meek of the earth, who have upheld His justice. Seek righteousness, seek humility. It may be that you will be hidden in the day of the Lord's anger.

Micah 6:8
He has shown you, O man, what is good; and what does the Lord require of you but to do justly, to love mercy, and to walk humbly with your God.

James 4:10
Humble yourselves in the sight of the Lord, and He will lift you up.

Philippians 2:3–5
Let nothing be done through selfish ambition or conceit, but in lowliness of mind let each esteem others better than himself. Let each one of you look out not only for his own interests, but also for the interests of others. Let this mind be in you which was also in Christ Jesus.

Proverbs 22:4
By humility and the fear of the Lord are riches and honor and life.

Proverbs 15:33
The fear of the Lord is the instruction of wisdom, and before honor is humility.

Psalm 147:6
The Lord lifts up the humble; He casts the wicked down to the ground.

Isaiah 57:15
For thus says the High and Lofty One, who inhabits eternity, whose name is Holy: I dwell in the high and holy place, with him who has a contrite and humble spirit, to revive the spirit of the humble, and to revive the heart of the contrite one.

Isaiah 66:2
"For all those things my hand has made, and all those things exist," says the Lord, "but on this one will I look: on him who is poor and of a contrite spirit, and who trembles at my word."

Titus 3:2
To speak evil of no one, to be peaceable, gentle, showing humility to all men.

This is how we are called to live.

Humility is an avenue of grace. 1 Peter 5:5. *Likewise, you younger people, submit yourselves to your elders. Yes, all of you be submissive to one another, and be clothed with humility, for God resists the proud, but gives grace to the humble.*

Humility allows us to be healed. 2 Chronicles 7:14. *If My people who are called by My name will humble themselves, and pray and seek My face, and turn from their wicked ways, then I will hear from heaven, and will forgive their sin and heal their land.*

Humility is an avenue of peace and freedom. 2 Timothy 2:24–26.*"And a servant of the Lord must not quarrel but be gentle to all, able to teach, patient, in humility, correcting those who are in opposition, if God perhaps will grant them repentance, so that they may know the truth, and that they may come to their senses and escape the snare of the devil, having been taken captive by him to do his will.*

The Pursuit of Humility

God casts such favour on humble believers. Humility is vital to a healthy relationship with Him and with others. This I know: a surrendered heart must always pursue humility. Look at the circumstances of your life right now; you may find yourself in one of three categories:

1. Becoming humbled
2. Being humble
3. Pursuing staying humble

Humility, in my opinion, is not something that comes and goes; it is an enduring quality. There are circumstances however, that can bring it, remind us of it, or help us keep it. It needs to be sought, found, and kept. The pursuit of humility may take us on a difficult road, but it worth its weight in gold, so to speak. Look at this quote from Mother Teresa: "Humility is the mother of all virtues—purity, charity, and obedience. It is in being humble that our love becomes real, devoted, and ardent. If you are humble, nothing will touch you, neither praise nor disgrace, because you know what you are. If you are blamed, you will not be discouraged. If they call you saint, you will not put yourself on a pedestal."

CHAPTER 9

Pride Rears Its Ugly Head

HUMILITY IS AN AVENUE TO THE HEART OF GOD, because it acts as a door, a bridge, and a channel to God's ways. Humility keeps our hearts open. The opposite, of course, would be closed hearts. Our beautiful struggle demands that we strive for humility and steer away from pride.

According to *Merriam-Webster's* dictionary, the definition of pride is the state or quality of being proud, inordinate self-esteem, an unreasonable conceit of one's own superiority in talents, beauty or wealth which manifests itself in lofty airs, distance, reserve, and often contempt of others.

Now let's take a few minutes to look at what happens when humility is *not* present. In some scriptures, God directly talks about both humility and pride at the same time. Pride is something that He has made a lot of references to; it is most definitely a hot topic of God's. Pride is the absolute opposite of humility. If anyone isn't convinced that humility is *not* the way to go, perhaps looking at what he has to say about pride will be a deterrent.

Proverbs 11:2
When pride comes, then comes shame; but with the humble is wisdom.

Proverbs 13:10
By pride comes nothing but strife, but with the well-advised is wisdom.

Proverbs 16:18
Pride goes before destruction and a haughty spirit before a fall.

Proverbs 29:23
A man's pride will bring him low but the humble in spirit will retain honour.

Daniel 5:20
But when his heart was lifted up and his spirit was hardened in pride, he was deposed from his kingly throne and they took his glory from him.

Mark 7:21–23
For from within, out of the heart of men, proceed evil thoughts, adulteries, fornications, murders, thefts, covetousness, wickedness, deceit, lewdness, an evil eye, blasphemy, pride, and foolishness. All these evil things come from within and defile a man.

God comes right out and says pride is evil! This really made me stop and take note. Remember, with humility there is a dependence on God. It makes sense then, that with pride there is a disconnect and an independence from God. This can easily lead to disobedience, which leads directly to not walking in His plan but our own, not receiving His blessings and certainly not living victoriously. Unfortunately, pride is very unrecognizable to most people. No one walks around saying "I am a proud fool." It shows up, instead, as things like judgement, blame, resentment, offense, greed, jealousy, fear, and disrespect for government and authority.

Think of pride as a glass wall, a distinct barrier. It is see-through yet impenetrable; because of its translucency it goes unnoticed by many (in fact, by most). A brick wall, on the other hand, would be obvious; if pride was like a brick wall, our lives would be more straight-forward. Unfortunately, this is not the case. The enemy has formulated pride as a glass wall, invisible to the naked eye and looking like protection to those who discover it. The only thing it seeks to protect is self—ego. Remember, that is a false identity. Our true identities are in Him.

The hypothetical prizes of pride are outright lies of the enemy that have us playing a game, not living life. Pride produces an illusion of control, a disconnect from God and others, and a self-dependency that keeps people spinning through life like a hamster on a wheel. It is impossible to live in true joy and to fulfill the insatiable desire for "happiness." That space in your gut that longs to be filled can only be filled by God. No thing, no person, no job, *nothing* can fill it. If you've been trying, you know it's true. Perhaps today is the day you will free yourself from the hamster wheel and just go to Him who knows you, and your needs, and your desires. Humility is what gets us there.

I meet many people who love God yet have not surrendered to Him, His will, and His ways. We need be "all in" to have total victory. One foot in heaven and one on earth puts a person on the fence and, well, lukewarm. God's desire for us is not that; it is for surrender and repentance and faith. *"So then, because you are lukewarm, and neither cold nor hot, I will vomit you out of My mouth. Because you say, 'I am rich, have become wealthy, and have need of nothing'—and do not know that you are wretched, miserable, poor, blind, and naked—I counsel you to buy from Me gold refined in the fire, that you may be rich; and white garments that you may be clothed, that the shame of your nakedness may not be revealed; and anoint your eyes with salve, that you may see. As many as I love, I rebuke and chasten. Therefore, be zealous and repent. Behold, I stand at the door and know. If anyone hears*

My voice and opens the door, I will come in to him and dine with him, and he with Me." (Revelation 3:16–20)

Perhaps we can dig in just a bit. I think it is safe to say that it is much easier to see or sense pride in someone else than in ourselves. It is also safe to say that prideful people typically look at others instead of themselves anyway. If you find yourself judging others, you may have an issue with pride. If you find yourself thinking that status shows who you are, you may have an issue with pride. If you find yourself obsessively worried about the future, you may have an issue with pride. If you find yourself staying the same and not growing, particularly in faith, you may have an issue with pride. If you have a me-first attitude, you may have an issue with pride. If you are always thinking, *What should I do about this?* you may have an issue with pride. If you wish to settle your own situations when someone has wronged you, you may have an issue with pride. If your outer person is more important than your inner person, you may have an issue with pride. If you believe that everything you think is correct, you may have an issue with pride. If you find you need to be in charge and control of things at home or work or in community, you may have an issue with pride. We could go on and on with life circumstances as examples, but I believe enough has been said to make the point.

The cycle of pride is very dangerous. Recognizing it early is important. Here is what happens: *Pride* (exaggeration of self) leads to an exaggeration of circumstances related to self, which leads to a *diluted* view of God and His role in our lives, which leads to a need to focus on ourselves to accomplish things and sustain what we started, which takes us back to the beginning, where *pride* is the force driving us. As if being in this cycle wasn't dangerous enough there is more; eventually, as we go around this cycle, God's influence becomes more and more diluted, until he is completely removed. This is one of the reasons why pride is such an effective tool of the enemy!

CHAPTER 10

To Serve, with Love

SERVING: TO ASSIST, AID AND SUPPLY. ALSO, TO LABOUR on behalf of or be in the service of another. *Service*: the action of helping or doing work for someone; favour, kindness. We can also talk about provision here. Service often entails the provision or equipping of things to people. We talked at length about God being the ultimate provider, perhaps we can look inward at how we fare at providing for others. The story in the beginning of the book where Jesus washed the disciples' feet is the ultimate story of serving and the attitude behind serving. Jesus told us it is an honour to serve, that He regards it as of the utmost importance and this section is here because of he emphasis he put on serving. May we all be the hands and feet of our Lord.

Serving Others

It is the will of God that we serve one another. James 2:8 tells us, *"If you really fulfill the royal law according to Scripture, 'You shall love your neighbor as yourself,' you do well."* Jesus showed us how to serve others; He taught us how by example and many times by word.

The disciples, too, reminded those they met of the importance of the way we treat one another. We are called to not only continually renew our minds and hearts and grow close to God, we are called to do good to those around us, whether in the body of Christ or not. God instructed that if our enemy is hungry we are to feed them (Proverbs 25:21–22); we are to help the widow (James 1:27) and allow God to use us as He sees fit to work in the Kingdom. Ephesians 2:10 says, *"For we are His workmanship, created in Christ Jesus for good works, which God prepared beforehand that we should walk in them."*

Looking back at the chosen scriptures, none of them specifically talked of serving. Yet Jesus took great care to be an example of it and to point it out, using the example of washing the disciples' feet (among many). Thus it is worthy enough to talk about. Serving, too, flows naturally to and from humility. In fact, serving is a natural occurrence in the identity we have in Him. There is a misconception that being a giver (serving) makes you weak. Jesus had a different point of view. He said that when we take care of others, we take care of Him. Matthew 25:34–40 tells of Jesus teaching in parables; it reads, *"Then the King will say to those on His right hand, 'Come, you blessed of my Father, inherit the kingdom prepared for you from the foundation of the world: for I was hungry and you gave Me food; I was thirsty and you gave Me drink; I was a stranger and you took Me in; I was naked and you clothed me; I was sick and you visited me; I was in prison and you came to Me.' Then the righteous will answer Him, saying 'Lord, when did we see You hungry and feed You, or thirsty and give You a drink? When did we see You a stranger and take You in, or naked and clothe You? Or when did we see You sick, or in prison and come to You?' And the King will answer and say to them, 'Assuredly, I say to you, inasmuch as you did it to one of the least of these, My brethren, you did it to Me.'"* Recounted in Acts 20:35, Jesus said, *"It is better to give than to receive."* Who can you give your time to? Your attention? Your understanding? Who do you know that just needs someone to talk to, someone to listen, and someone to care?

We can also do ourselves and everyone we meet a favour and know that *everyone* has a story. We need to make a paradigm shift in our thinking and always bear this in mind. Sometimes serving God and others is simply and truly showing patience, peacefulness, and mercy. We shouldn't need the details. We don't have to get it. We don't need to understand. Just think about how you would wish to be treated. The golden rule has never gone out of style. Paul wrote it like this in 2 Corinthians 1:3–4: *"Blessed be the God and Father of our Lord Jesus Christ, the Father of mercies and God of all comfort, who comforts us in all our tribulation, that we may be able to comfort those who are in any trouble, with the comfort with which we ourselves are comforted by God."* Also, in Galatians 6:1–2, we read, *"Brethren, if a man is overtaken in any trespass, you who are spiritual restore such a one in a spirit of gentleness, considering yourself lest you also be tempted. Bear one another's burdens, and so fulfil the law of Christ."* And from John, comes this gem: *"My little children, let us not love in word or in tongue, but in deed and in truth."* (1 John 3:18)

Further, Hebrews 10:24–25 says, *"And let us consider one another in order to stir up love and good works, not forsaking the assembling of ourselves together, as is the manner of some, but exhorting one another, and so much the more as you see the Day approaching."* And in Proverbs 3:27 we read, *"Do not withhold good from those to whom it is due, when it is in the power of your hand to do so."*

Paul demonstrates perfectly what we have been discussing. Humility and serving go hand in hand and are key in "walking out" our faith. Serving is one of the activities we do to show that we belong to Him. Here it is from his letter to the Romans (Romans 12:1–21), titled "The Cheerful Giver":

I beseech you therefore, brethren, by the mercies of God that you present your bodies a living sacrifice, holy, acceptable to God, which is your reasonable service. And do not be conformed to this world, but be transformed by the renewing of your mind, that you may prove what is good and acceptable and perfect will of God. For I say, through the grace given to me, to everyone who is among you, not to think of himself more highly than he ought to, but to think soberly, as God has dealt to each one a measure of faith. For as we have many members in one body, but all the members do not have the same function, so we being many are one body in Christ and individually members of one another. Having then gifts differing according to the grace that is given to us, let us use them: if prophecy, let us prophesy in proportion to our faith, or ministry, let us use it in our ministering, he who teaches, in teaching, he who exhorts, in exhortation, he who gives, with liberality, he who leads, with diligence, he who shows mercy, with cheerfulness.

Let love be without hypocrisy. Abhor what is evil. Cling to what is good. Be kindly, affectionate to one another with brotherly love, in honor giving preference to one another, not lagging in diligence, fervent in spirit, serving the Lord, rejoicing in hope, patient in tribulation, continuing steadfastly in prayer, distributing to the needs of the saints, given to hospitality.

Bless those who persecute you, bless and do not curse. Rejoice with those who rejoice, and weep with those who weep. Be of the same mind toward one another. Do not set your mind on high things, but associate with the humble. Do not be wise in your own opinion.

Repay no one evil for evil. Have regard for good things in the sight of all men. If it is possible, as much as depends on you, live peaceably with all men. Beloved, do not avenge yourselves, but rather give place to wrath, for it is written, "Vengeance is mine, I will repay," says the Lord. Therefore, if your enemy is hungry, feed him. If he is thirsty, give him a drink. For in so doing you will heap coals of fire on his head. Do not overcome by evil, but overcome evil with good.

Perhaps this is a good time to make a mental or written note on what we can do for other people. I know, as I know in my Knower, that through that portion God was pressing into your spirit people and ideas. When He does that, we must be diligent to follow the instructions. We usually form one layer in a multi-layered event or time for someone else. Let us not miss ours! We spoke of obedience earlier, and it is imperative that we aim for a timely and obedient following of what God calls us to do. Remember, we serve in two ways: we serve others, and we serve God. Most of the time, though, we serve others by serving God. Let's explore this further.

Serving God

As people are miraculously changed, a natural inclination to serve takes place—to serve people, yes, but to serve God more. We lose ourselves in the marvel and wonder of how amazing God truly is; we fall in love with being obedient, and we wish to serve Him. It just happens that way. There is a releasing of old junk and a fresh intake of splendour that is love—that is, God. If this is not the case for you today, it can be; it will be. Serving draws us near, keeps us close, and earns us crowns in heaven. Our salvation alone validates the desire, and the need, to serve Him. Look at Luke 1:74–75: *"To grant us that we, being delivered from the hand of our enemies, might serve Him without fear, in holiness and righteousness before Him all the days of our life."*

There was a sentence in "The Cheerful Giver" excerpt that said, *"I beseech you therefore, brethren, by the mercies of God that you present your bodies a living sacrifice, holy, acceptable to God, which is your reasonable service."* Take note of those last five words! We are expected to give ourselves and live lives of service to God. He wants to work through us in others. He wishes us to be examples of love and kindness that draw others to Him. He so desires that we be His hands, feet, and voice in our families and communities and in the world. And He asks that we do it not just in deed but from our humbled and surrendered hearts. James 2:14–16 reads, *"What does it profit, my brethren, if someone says he has faith but does not have works? Can faith save him? If a brother or sister is naked and destitute of daily food, and one of you says to them, 'Depart in peace, be warmed and filled,' but you do not give them the things which are needed for the body, what does it profit?"* This scripture talks of works that put action to our faith. I believe we are to serve others, as taught in Scripture. Yet it's true that we serve God as well. Separating the two may seem futile, but it is to fix attention on the source. I see it like this: we hold doors open, help people with groceries, and we donate food to shelters; we may even cook for people and walk their dogs. Most of the little things we do as we serve others we don't ask God about, and we don't get direct word from Him to do so. We simply, out of the goodness of our hearts and the desire to serve, do nice things for others. There are times, however, when this is not the case. There are times when God gives us clear directions about an action that He wants us to do with or for a certain person.

I would now like to ask you, "Is there something that God has been asking you to do for someone (or for Him) that you have been putting off? Are you willing to do it now?" Would you be willing to lay down some pride? Serve a neighbour? Prepare a meal? Share Christ? Forgive someone? Forgive yourself?

Serving creates a bond of community in the Body of Christ—and beyond. It binds us to Him as we, in his likeness, do what He did. It also binds us to each other as we carry others' burdens, lighten others' yokes, and brighten others' hearts. The most important heart we brighten is God's, as He watches us give up a bit of ourselves for other's sake, even if only for a few moments at a time. Remember the promises and enjoy the blessings. Give, serve, and walk humbly to His open arms. I think this is passage from Mark 12:30–31 is fitting: *"And you shall love the Lord God with all your heart, with all your soul, with all your mind, and with all your strength. This is the first commandment. And the second, like it, is this: You shall love your neighbor as yourself. There is no commandment greater than these."*

When in doubt, see if what you are doing (or not doing) measures anywhere near this. We are truly expected to learn and grow as Christians and then to do something about it. 2 Timothy 3:16–17 says, *All Scripture is given by inspiration of God, and is profitable for doctrine, for reproof, for correction, for instruction in righteousness, that the man of God may be complete, thoroughly equipped for every good work.* Resting on our laurels, so to speak, really isn't expected; good works are.

Our goal should be to bring honour to Him by our lives, which includes our works and our good deeds to those around us. It is important, though, that we stay humble and that we keep a level head about what we do, particularly when we have been instructed by God, *"Take heed that you do not do your charitable deeds before men, to be seen by them. Otherwise you have no reward from your Father in heaven. Therefore, when you do a charitable deed, do not sound a trumpet before you as the hypocrites do in the synagogues and in the streets, that they may have glory from men. Assuredly, I say to you, they have their reward. But when you do a charitable deed, do not let your left hand know what your right hand is doing, that your charitable deed may be done in secret; and your Father who sees in secret will Himself reward you openly."* (Matthew 6:1–4)

A Servant's Blessings

For those who have servants' hearts and who adopt a humble disposition toward serving, there are beautiful promises to look forward to. Let's look at the ways serving blesses us, the doers.

Serving God keeps us close to Him. *"If anyone serves me, let him follow me; and where I am there my servant will also be. If anyone serves me, him my Father will honour."* (John 12:26)

Serving keeps us humble in attitude. *"But not so among you, on the contrary, he who is greatest among you, let him be as the younger, he who governs, as he who serves. For who is greater, he who sits at the table, or he who serves? Is it not he who sits at the table? Yet I am among you as the One who serves."* (Luke 22:26–27)

"For you, brethren, have been called to liberty; only do not use liberty as an opportunity for the flesh, but through love serve one another." (Galatians 5:13)

We are also blessed to inherit the kingdom of God. *"Therefore, since we are receiving a kingdom which cannot be shaken, let us have grace, by which we may serve God acceptably with reverence and godly fear."* (Hebrews 12:28)

As for me, when I see Him face to face, I want to hear Him say, "Well done, My good and faithful servant!"

PRINCIPLES 4 AND 5: GRATITUDE AND WORSHIP

CHAPTER 11

Attitude of Gratitude

WHEN I BEGAN THIS BOOK, WHEN IT WAS IN ITS infancy, I questioned the flow and where things fit, etc. God gave the principles to me in this order, and they've never been changed. I had a feeling that the original order made sense, but as I write, that sense has solidified. When we depend on God, we are naturally drawn to a more humbled nature; we are inclined to do more things for people than ever, and our hearts tend to fill with praises and thanksgiving—especially as we remember where we came from (as a matter of the heart, not of geography). We are rounding down to the last two principles, and I feel as though I am at the top of a roller coaster—I am so excited! At this very moment it's very early morning, still dark. I can hear the rustle of the leaves and the rain on the roof through the open kitchen window, where I sit and write before my family gets up.

I am overcome this morning not only with excitement to see this book come to completion but also with joy and humility and gratitude. I feel joy because He loves and cherishes me. I am humbled that He chose me. The gratitude I feel right now is because He used *me*. I am still in awe of what He has done in me and through me, and we are just getting started! This is exactly what I want for everyone—for you. I want the transformation in your life to be so unbelievable and miraculous that all you want to do is give back such gratitude and worship that you would offer your life. I want everyone to give their lives as an offering, that everything we do may be for His glory. Gratitude helps us live from the inside out; it is a shield that prevents people from living from the outside in. Gratitude helps us live lives that are exploding with all the good things of God, rather than imploding with all the negative things in the world in the haste of day after day. It makes us stop and smell the roses.

Looking back at the scripture from Luke 17:11–16, we read, *"Now it happened as He went to Jerusalem that he passed through the midst of Samaria and Galilee. Then as He entered a certain village, there met him ten men who were lepers, who stood afar off. And they lifted up their voices and said, 'Jesus, Master, have mercy on us!' So, when He saw them, he said to them, 'Go, show yourselves to the priests.' And so it was that as they went, they were cleansed. And one of them, when he saw that he was healed, returned, and with a loud voice glorified God, and fell down on his face at His feet, giving Him thanks. And he was a Samaritan."*

So, as the story goes, nine men were healed. I think it would be reasonable to say that they were bursting with happiness and much pleased, considering they had asked to be healed in the first place. The story does not say how far they went. I imagine some went quite a distance. What is interesting to me is that only one came back; only one healed man out of the ten decided to go back and give thanks. These men were not just sick, they were outcasts. Their disease would have affected their bodies, minds, and way of life. What must happen for some of us to get into gratitude? What needs to take place in our lives for us to shift our thinking to that realm of thankfulness? Remember our talk about humility and how it is an attitude? Well, so is gratitude. The outward "attitude of gratitude" that brought the one healed leper back is example enough. I wish we had heard more about his life after this story.

We are going to explore gratitude as an *emotion* and gratitude as it brings about *action*. Let's explore how we can live victoriously and abundantly, full of life with gratitude, not just feeling it but acting on it. A kind thought or feeling toward someone else is rendered useless if we keep it to ourselves. It's like wrapping up a present and never giving it away. Giving, especially giving thanks, is crucial for a balanced perspective. It helps us stay focused with intention to follow God. Gratitude diffuses the sting of the past and makes the present day what it really is—good. No matter what circumstances we live in, gratitude is an option, a choice, and a necessity.

Gratitude is "the quality or feeling of being grateful or thankful." In the scriptures, not just the ones used for this study, but in *all* Scripture, the words *grateful* and *gratitude* are not found, but the word *thankful* is.

Gratefulness = Thankfulness

Digging into the scriptures, there are many (over one hundred) verses directly related to the act of *giving thanks*. I find it interesting that gratitude is directly paired with *action* in Scripture. Gratitude is an attitude of the heart that requires action. Think of gratitude as the key that unlocks the door and sets people free from misery, depression, jealousy, fear, and resentment, to name a few. Gratitude forces us to look *up*, not *out*. It also is key in keeping a surrendered heart wide open! It is impossible to feel love (faith) and fear at the same time. It is equally impossible to feel gratitude and disappointment at the same time.

Let's talk about some easy stuff up front. Being thankful is probably something every single person would say they had experienced. Gratitude is generally known, and expected, especially of Christ followers. Let's now explore how we can implement it in our everyday lives, our personal lives, and our status quo. Let's do a quick exercise to get our brains and hearts warmed up.

Write down as many things as possible that you are grateful for right now. Use the margin. Use a journal. Use a paper. Use your hand. Use anything you can write on. Gratitude is an action word. Just do it!

The Broken Bible, the Gift Card, and More Than One Blessing

I'm going to tell you a story. I love this story: I love the circumstances, the lesson, and the blessings. I wish to share it because it is so simple that it's easy to miss in everyday life. I bet we all have these kinds of opportunities; we just need to hone in on them, be open to listening to the gentle voice of God, and then act on them. A few years ago, while I was teaching this as a study, I was on my way to the church. It was April, a beautiful spring morning, still cool, but I could see the promise of renewal everywhere as I was drove along the long and twisty road to where I was headed for the morning lesson. The study was broken up into four weeks, and we were on week three—gratitude. As I was driving, I was visualizing how some of the morning might go. I knew that we were going to do the above exercise, and I decided that I should give a reward to the person who could come up with the longest list of things they were grateful for. I was thinking I should stop and pick up something appropriate on the way. What should I get? I was excited, because I love to give gifts. As the sun shone and I was dreaming a bit of how fun this could all really be, I felt God tugging at me to use a gift card that I had in my wallet. Not too long before this, a good friend of mine had given me a gift certificate to my favourite Christian book store. I had it tucked in my wallet and was saving it to use on a new bible. My favourite bible, which I had been using for about twelve years, was literally in three pieces. I desperately needed a new one, and that gift card was just the ticket. So I was a bit confused (and sad) when God asked me to give it to someone else. "But, Lord, you know how much I need a new bible. I will stop and get another gift." Still, I felt Him strongly wanting me to give it. Finally, I gave in. "Okay," I said. Once I relented, I became excited to see how He would use it. I absolutely love being a part of something cool and orchestrated by God.

Before the exercise, I announced that there was a gift card as a prize for the lady who had written the most down. I shared the story of my morning drive, my conversation with God, and my slight unwillingness to part with the gift card, as it was clear I needed a new bible. I held up my tattered bible as proof and got a few chuckles. It really was in bad shape. After the exercise, I gave the card to the lady with the longest list, giving her also a huge smile and ginormous hug. I was happy to see someone rewarded for being so grateful. It was a good day.

The following week I went to present the last principle—worship. After it was presented, the lady who had won the gift card came up to me with a very large gift bag. Remember, I love giving gifts, but who doesn't absolutely love to *get* them? "Tammy, I have something for you," she said.

"For me?" Indeed, another good day! We found a spot for me to open the bag; in it was a beautiful new bible. It was a pink leather-bound NKJV bible. "Omigosh, this is awesome!" The gift someone had given me had become a gift to this woman, and it then became a gift to me again. We both got blessed when she used the card I gave her to give me the exact thing I needed. Isn't God amazing! Instead of me going to my favourite book store and buying a bible, God used that simple little gift card to acknowledge and bless someone for their gratitude and let them be a blessing to me. In the end, I got the bible in God's way and time, and He got all the glory. Yes!

I understood the concept, the truth, and the necessity of gratitude to the heart and soul. I understood the positive energy and vibration gratitude gives. I valued the teaching and have lived the benefits. Recently, though, I've felt there was more. I started asking *why*. Why does gratitude change so much? What I have learned is this; *that gratitude (in action) validates people to the core.* The truth we must all know is that we are created for community and connection with others. This kind of outward living in and from a place of gratitude strengthens those bonds when we esteem others. Saying thank you in any way, shape, or form is simple, yet powerful. Send a card, make a phone call, smile, hug, bake a cake, make some soup—do whatever it takes. Just do it.

Gratitude is also intricately woven into the concepts of humility and serving; they seem to all be crucial pieces of the same big-picture puzzle we all call life. My prayer and goal in all of this is to change that slightly (or dramatically) to the puzzle we call victorious life. Gratitude changes our perspective. Gratitude changes our outlook. Gratitude changes the energy field we broadcast. Gratitude changes the intention with which we go about our days. Much research has been done on the benefits of gratitude. It has been shown to bring people better relationships, better sleep, less anxiety and gastrointestinal symptoms related to it, improved capacity for compassion, and reduced anger and bitterness, allowing forgiveness. It has been written that it "unlocks the fullness of life." I must agree.

Gratitude is not a new concept though; people have been writing about it for centuries. While I am focusing mostly on Scripture, amazing people have understood the model of gratitude. Ralph Waldo Emerson said this: "Cultivate the habit of being grateful for every good thing that comes to you, and give thanks continuously. And because all things have contributed to your advancement, you should include all things in your gratitude." John Milton said, "Gratitude bestows reverence, allowing us to encounter everyday epiphanies, those transcendent moments of awe that change forever how we experience life and the world." So beautiful! Doesn't that quote completely sum up—much more eloquently—what we just discussed? It absolutely does! John Milton was a poet who lived in the 1600s and Ralph Waldo Emerson lived in the 1800s, but their words are important today, because the essence of people has never changed.

We talked previously about how we can *know* and *rely* on God's Word, His character, and the aspects we can depend on Him for. Here are some of the things Scripture says we can be grateful for:

Everything, All the Time

We read in 1Thessalonians 5:16–18, *"Rejoice always, pray without ceasing, in everything give thanks; for this is the will of God in Christ Jesus for you."* This pretty much says it all, right, everything in one sentence? But what does it really mean? After my car accident, I questioned some things; I questioned purpose and reason. I questioned why—for about five minutes. (Yes, it was a bit longer than five minutes, but it wasn't long.) Gratitude is a choice. *Always* means no matter what, no matter when. Easier said than done? Absolutely. It's a tall order—but it is the order!

Ultimately, if I trust God and His ways and I am surrendered to them, I can be thankful for it all. Why? Because He can and will use it all for my good if I choose to accept that truth. (Romans 8:28: *"And we know that all things work together for good to those who love God, to those who are called according to His purpose."*)

Growing up, most of us learned to label circumstances and times as good or bad, negative or positive. The truth is that we really have no idea what is good or bad, because it all can and does work for the greater good. At first I labelled my car accident as bad. Almost two years later, I can testify to how God used it for His greater good, and while I don't recommend crashing into a tree, I do recommend taking a step back and holding off from labelling things. God either is ordaining things or allowing things, and either way it all filters through His beautiful hands. I am alluding to His sovereignty as the big picture. We can't know, nor do we need to know, all the details. He knows them, and He has us in the palm of His hand. What we need to do is go back to chapter one, about depending on God. We need to be willing to put our money where our mouth is and surrender already. In the meantime, we should be grateful for it all. James says it like this: *"My brethren, count it all joy when you fall into various trials, knowing that the testing of your faith produces patience."* (James 1:2–3)

Being grateful is half of the equation of gratitude. The other half is the acting on it. Gratitude in action makes major impacts in the larger world, because it makes major impacts in *our world*. We can change the larger world we see and live in by changing the world we immediately see and live in. Humility, serving, faith, and gratitude are attitudes that drive us to do something. They are action driven, and they are full of energy. There is a direct correlation to giving, serving, and acting in kindness generated from gratitude that leads to having an abundant life, without reference to money or material goods. The flow of God's blessings pours on humble and grateful hearts. The concept of "you reap what you sow" is what we are talking about.

Ephesians 5:17–20 tells us, *"Therefore do not be unwise, but understand what the will of the Lord is. And do not be drunk with wine, in which is dissipation; but be filled with the Spirit, speaking to one another in psalms and hymns and spiritual songs, singing and making melody in your heart to the Lord, giving thanks always for all things to God the Father in the name of our Lord Jesus Christ."* And Colossians 3:17 says, *"And whatever you do in word or deed, do all in the name of the Lord Jesus, giving thanks to God the Father through Him."*

Paul articulates what we are talking about in the opposite way in his letter to the Philippians. I like to look at things from both sides, and this is very fitting: *"Do all things without complaining and disputing, that you may become blameless and harmless children of God without fault in the midst of a crooked and perverse generation, among whom you shine as lights in the world."* (Philippians 2:14)

Our Faith

Let's go back a minute to recount something, whilst remembering faith. Faith is a spiritual gift, according to 1 Corinthians 12:4–11. *"There are diversities of gifts, but the same Spirit. There are differences of ministries, but the same Lord. And there are diversities of activities, but it is the same God who works all in all. But the manifestation of the Spirit is given to each one for the profit of all: for to one is given the word of wisdom through the Spirit, to another the word of knowledge through the same Spirit, to another faith by the same Spirit, to another gifts of healings by the same Spirit, to another the working of miracles, to another prophecy, to another discerning of spirits, to another different kinds of tongues, to another the interpretation of tongues. But one and the same Spirit works all these things, distributing to each one individually as He wills."*

So, there are many gifts, and we each have one (or many). Being grateful for faith alone would rock a lot of worlds! Can you imagine what would happen if you professed daily, "I am grateful for my exceeding portions of grace and faith and the blessings they bring." I dare you!

Faith of Others

In 2 Thessalonians 1:3 we read, *"We are bound to thank God always for you, brethren, as it is fitting, because your faith grows exceedingly, and the love of every one of you all abounds toward each other."*

Romans 1:8 explains, *"First, I thank my God through Jesus Christ for you all, that your faith is spoken of throughout the whole world. For God is my witness, whom I serve with my spirit in the gospel of His Son, that without ceasing I make mention of you always in my prayers, making request if by some means, now at last I may find a way in the will of God to come to you. For I long to see you, that I may impart to you some spiritual gift, so that you may be established—that is, that I may be encouraged together with you by the mutual faith both of you and me."*

It is important to be grateful for the faith of others, to recognize that our walk is the walk of others and that we shine our light in, through, and around those near us. As we read this today, we can be greatly encouraged to share, learn, and grow while watching others in their faith walks. Like cheerleaders on the sidelines, we all need to give encouragement, in word, deed, and voice. If we have people praying over us and for us, this concept makes more sense. Other people engaging their faith for us and toward us is one of the most beautiful things we can experience, and it should not be taken for granted but highly appreciated.

I am so grateful for the faith of the women around me. When things get heavy, I know I can reach out and say, "Prayers, please!" I know without a doubt that they have my back; details are not necessary. They go to battle for me, lifting me up to God. I can feel it, and its comfort is wonderful. During those difficult times when I haven't even processed what's happening but I am smack in the middle of a mess, those prayers are hitting God's ears in the meantime. My reaching out allows them to intercede for me, and God hears those prayers on my behalf. Knowing that you're in someone's prayers, that others count on God for you, is amazing. What a blessing to have that—and to be that for someone else.

The Lord's Mercies

Psalm 100:4
Enter into His gates with thanksgiving, and into His courts with praise. Be thankful to Him and bless His name.

Psalm 103:1–5
Bless the Lord, O my soul; and all that is within me, bless His holy name! Bless the Lord, O my soul, and forget not all His benefits; who forgives all your iniquities, Who heals all your diseases, Who redeems your life from

destruction, Who crowns you with lovingkindness and tender mercies, Who satisfies your mouth with good things, so that your youth is renewed like the eagle's.

Psalm 136:14
Oh, give thanks to the Lord, for He is good! For His mercy endures forever. Oh, give thanks to the God of gods! For his mercy endures forever. Oh, give thanks to the Lord of lords! For His mercy endures forever: to Him who alone does great wonders, for His mercy endures forever.

Jeremiah 32:1718
Ah, Lord God! Behold, You have made the heavens and the earth by Your great power and outstretched arm. There is nothing too hard for you. You show lovingkindness to thousands and repay the iniquity of the fathers into the bosom of their children after them—the Great, the Mighty God, whose name is the Lord of hosts.

God's Grace
Looking back to the scripture of "The Cheerful Giver" (this is just back in the Serving Others section) the last line holds something that should be mentioned. *"Thanks be to God for His indescribable gifts."* Paul is referring to God's exceeding grace from the preceding sentence. Acting on your grateful heart is a sure and fast way to receive God's grace!

Jesus's Example

Previously we talked about Jesus being an example of serving and humility as He washed the disciples' feet. Today let's take note of His example of gratitude, looking at how and how often He gave thanks. Remember, we are talking about gratitude as an *action word*, not just an *emotion*.

Matthew 15:36
And He took the seven loaves and the fish and gave thanks, broke them and gave them to His disciples; and the disciples gave to the multitude.

Matthew 26:27
Then He took the cup and gave thanks, and gave it to them saying, "Drink from it, all of you."

John 11:38–44
Then Jesus, again groaning in Himself, came to the tomb. It was a cave, and a stone lay against it. Jesus said, "Take away the stone." Martha, the sister of him who was dead, said to Him, "Lord, by this time there is a stench, for he has been dead for four days." Jesus said to her, "Did I not say to you that if you would believe you would see the glory of God?" Then they took away the stone from the place where the dead man was lying. And Jesus lifted up His eyes and said, "Father, I thank you that you have heard me. And I know that you always hear me, but because of the people who are standing by I said this, that they may believe that you sent me." Now, when He had said these things, He cried with a loud voice, "Lazarus, come forth!" And he who had died came out, bound hand and foot with grave clothes, and his face was wrapped with a cloth, Jesus said to them, "Loose him, and let him go."

It is very interesting to me that Jesus gave thanks *before* He performed His miracles. This kind of attitude is contrary to what we typically see. Most of us are thankful *after* we get something we want or when something goes our way. I am suggesting we look at his amazing example of gratitude. Jesus is grateful to even have the opportunity to pray and to be heard. Are we? Do we even understand this concept? I am talking to myself here too. It's easy to get into the groove of prayer and Godly conversation and forget what a privilege it really is. Jesus's gratitude radiates from His being—prior to miracles. Wow! Gratitude opens the door—no, the floodgates—of blessing and opportunity.

About this thing called gratitude, sometimes we are challenged to feel it, and especially to *choose* it. Life happens. Life hurts. If we function on the plane of feeling how things seem or are, then we are in for some major drama. The challenge is to choose how we want to feel and then go after it. Not feeling very grateful? The intervention is called a paradigm shift, a change in our thinking that allows a different perspective to drive our actions. There are some things we can do to get us back in line with it. We can *re-engage* our gratitude, we can *up* the level of our gratitude, and we can *jump-start* our gratitude by doing something very purposefully. Going back to the list is crucial here! Challenge yourself to read it every day as a reminder. Challenge yourself to add to it or rewrite it weekly, and make sure it's longer.

Once we start with a mindset of gratitude, it is sure to grow, because we are open and searching. God can and will guide our hearts on this one, because He loves to be part of our everyday lives. How honoured would He be if we shared this with Him instead of just the hurts? My husband and I start every morning with prayer, and that prayer starts with "Thank you." We are grateful that we can talk to him about what He has done and is doing in our lives and family. I must add, though, that we are also grateful for what He *will* do—for what's coming, for His amazing plans for us, for the blessings and the lessons and the freedom and mercy He will pour out over us. We are especially grateful when we see prayers answered and blessings come to pass. Even when things seem stagnant, we know He is working on the sidelines to bring something to pass.

Grateful hearts act! Those acts of kindness please God, and His abundant blessings pour on us to do more great works. The fruit of the works not only blesses others, but they bless the doers just as much. It may even be true that they bless us more.

Gratitude Is

Gratitude is
The voice of love,
    The sound of acceptance,
        The attitude of faith,
            Surrender to the unknown.

It is the line in the sand,
    The here and now,
        The square one of everyone's life;
Of new and of old,
    Of what is to be.
Gratitude serves others
    And you,
        Essentially.

Unequivocally and fundamentally,
    It opens the heart,
        Feeds the spirit,
            Frees the dreams,
                And sets fire inside our deepest passions.

Gratitude is the giver
    Of love
        And is the builder
            Of bridges;
                It is the open road of acceptance.
It is core,
    It is key,
        And it is real.

Gratitude helps us feel and heal
    What is past
        And to seal what is to come.
It is the glue and the bond
    Of people
        And of our truest selves.

It is humbling and serving and giving.
Gratitude is a choice;
> It is our voice from within.
> —Tammy Tassone (2013)

CHAPTER 12

Worship

Who, What, When, Where, Why, and How

WE ARE GOING TO EXPLORE THE LAST OF THE FIVE principles: worship. Several of the scriptures we started with demonstrate the *attitude* of worship.

The Story of Mary and Martha

This is from Luke 10:38–42. *"Now it happened as they went that He entered a certain village, and a certain woman named Martha welcomed Him into her house. And she had a sister called Mary, who also sat at Jesus' feet and heard his word. But Martha was distracted with much serving, and she approached Him and said, 'Lord, do you not care that my sister has left me to serve alone? Therefore tell her to help me.' And Jesus answered and said to her, 'Martha, Martha, you are worried and troubled about many things. But one thing is needed, and Mary has chosen that good part, which will not be taken away from her.'"*

Countless times I can recall being in my kitchen when my then-little children, completely oblivious to the tasks at hand, were sitting at my feet or even *on* my feet, rendering me incapable of even taking a step. All they wanted was to be near. They would sit happily in my presence. They felt complete *faith*, complete *trust*, and complete *dependency*. (I think we just came full circle!) Where else would they be? And where else should *we* be but at Jesus's feet, in complete faith, trust, and dependency? Just to be in his presence—*ahhhhhhh!*

Worship is such an integral part of our faith. Sometimes it is quiet, sometimes our worship is full of song, sometimes we are alone, and sometimes we are in a chorus of hundreds or thousands. Worshipping Jesus isn't just saying, "I believe you are Lord and Saviour, and thank you for loving me." It's really *living out* the process of our faith.

The stronger my faith has become, the more means I find to worship. The more I have come to know Him and surrender to Him, the more I seek Him. The more I seek Him the more I find him, the more I know; the more I know the more I worship.

So, dig in and seek to find Him. Find Him and go through the process. Dig into gratitude and worship. Together these two things can blow a heart wide open. If you want miracles, dive into these, whether you feel it or not, and you will see Him show up!

Let's look at what worship is, the power that worship brings to our spiritual lives, and the way to be a true worshipper. As we found the correlation between the words *gratitude* and *thankfulness*, we will also be using the word *praise* interchangeably with *worship*. Being in awe of God—that's where worship is!

Know this: Godly encounters lead us straight to worship. And worship leads us straight to Godly encounters! Ezekiel 36:26 reads, *"I will give you a new heart and put a new spirit within you; I will take the heart of stone out of your flesh and give you a heart of flesh."* It is this new heart that allows us to see God as being worthy of our praise. The new heart in us helps us to understand worship. As we seek Him and live out daily our surrendered lives, we find ourselves in the middle of the most beautiful divine relationship with the One who created the universe.

Worship, according to the dictionary version, is reverent honour and homage paid to God. Simply put, it is giving due worth to God. We could call it worth-ship or worthiness.

True worship is the result of the created's response in love to the Creator. It's really a revelation of the power of the cross and our response to it. Instead of seeking God and God alone to fill us, people seek experiences. They come up short when these experiences don't fill the void as people thought they would. We are made to be connected to God, and worshipping is wired into us. God wants our hearts. He wants true and full worship from our hearts, not just in voice and deed. Look at Amos 5:21–24, which says, *"I hate, I despise your feast days, and I do not savor your sacred assemblies. Though you offer Me burnt offerings and your grain offerings, I will not accept them nor will I regard your fattened peace offerings. Take away from me the noise of your songs, for I will not hear the melody of your stringed instruments. But let justice run down like water and righteousness like a mighty stream."* He wants us. Come as you are. Give it all to Him.

Worship is not an event; it is not an experience—it is experienced! Worship is something we are, something we live, in the truest part of our being. Worship is about the glory of God, and it identifies the Kingdom we belong to. John 4:24 says, *"God is spirit, and those who worship Him must worship in spirit and truth."*

We looked at the story of the man who was cured of leprosy along with nine others. He was the only one who went back to thank Jesus for healing him. He wasn't asking for anything; he was totally worshipping Jesus and being grateful. Again, we get the question about humility and serving—which comes first? Now I am wondering about gratitude and worship. Does worshipping make you more grateful, or does being grateful cause you to worship? It's a thought to ponder. Either way, they are strongly connected.

Psalm 68:3–4
But let the righteous be glad; let them rejoice before God; yes, let them rejoice exceedingly. Sing to God, sing praises to his name; extol Him who rides on the clouds, by His name YAH, and rejoice before Him.

Psalm 98:6–7
Oh come, let us worship and bow down; let us kneel before the Lord our Maker. For He is our God, and we are the people of His pasture, and the sheep of His hand.

Ephesians 3:20–21
Now to Him who is able to do exceedingly abundantly above all that we ask or think, according to the power that works in us, to Him be glory in the church by Christ Jesus to all generations, forever and ever. Amen.

Psalm 63:1–8
O God, You are my God; early will I seek You; my soul thirsts for You; my flesh longs for You in a dry and thirsty land where there is no water. So I have looked for You in the sanctuary, to see Your power and Your glory. Because Your lovingkindness is better than life, my lips shall praise You. Thus I will bless You while I live; I will lift up my hands in Your name. My soul shall be satisfied as with marrow and fatness, and my mouth shall praise You with joyful lips. When I remember You on my bed, I meditate on You in the night watches. Because You have been my help, therefore in the shadow of Your wings I will rejoice. My soul follows close behind You; Your right hand upholds me." This is the kind of worship we are talking about!

Isaiah 43:21
This people I have formed for Myself; they shall declare My praise.

We are called to give glory to God in all we say and do. Above all, God, who already has all the glory, should receive all the glory from us. Apart from Him we can do nothing, which means that all that we do is in Him and through Him. In humility we know that whatever we accomplish, it is God who gets the glory, not us. I've added this here because worship is not something that we *do* but something we *are*. Yes, we sing, attend church, pray, sit quietly in nature—there are all kinds of things we do in our worship—but they are only a part of it. Our lives, in essence, *are* worship; at least that is the goal. If we give glory to God in all we say and do, I think it is directly related to worship. When we surrender to God, we are in worship. When we pray, abide, and are obedient, we are in worship. Our whole lives are acts of worship as we take our love and awe to His throne and offer them.

God Wants Our Hearts

Romans 12:1
I beseech you therefore, brethren, by the mercies of God, that you present your bodies a living sacrifice, holy, acceptable to God, which is your reasonable service.

John 4:23–24
But the hour is coming, and now is, when the true worshippers will worship the Father in spirit and truth; for the Father is seeking such to worship Him.

True and authentic worship means a surrendered heart. When we pray and connect to God and love Him with all we have, we are worshipping. When we pray for and connect to others and serve them, we are worshipping. Essentially, we worship God with our whole lives. This is a huge reality check for me. When we look back at identifying ourselves in Christ, being humbled by that identity, serving in that, and then *choosing* to be grateful in that—worship is taking all of that and going deeper.

Worship is bringing before God that which is real and true and valuable from our hearts. Remember we talked about God meeting us where we are? He meets us right there in moments of worship. We only need to bring what we have. When I come back to the truth of the cross, I am in awe, and my heart wants to worship. There are so many other things that cause this—being forgiven, observing nature, having prayer answered, etc. Worship is something we do in the moments of realizing the mercy and love of God. True worship is our simplest and most beautiful response to Him.

The Power of Worship

Worship keeps us connected to God. We grant true surrender and openness in those moments or times of worship. Does anyone have trouble with the whole concept of surrender? Then start praising God and see what happens. When we are given the choice, it is always better to *worship* then to *whine*. God knows our hearts already, and worshipping promotes good; whining does not. When we really understand the value of worship, it helps us stand strong. Think about David's psalms. In the middle of complete anguish, he took time to step back and praised God. We could all take note of this great example. During hard times it may be difficult to praise God for the challenges we are facing, but it can be easy to praise Him for being Him, for all the things He has done so far, and for all the things He will do in/for us yet. We don't always *feel* that we want to worship. The truth is, though, that worship is exactly what we need to do to change our thinking and *focus*. Worship, like gratitude, is a choice we make.

Worship is simply a *lifestyle* and an *attitude* of the heart. True worship converts us to His temple, and moments of worship become the lifestyle God calls us to. God knows He is amazing; what matters is that we know it and that we show Him. Worship proves to God that we know who He is, and it is our response to Him. Sing praises, sing praises—no matter how that looks.

Remember that we spoke earlier about surrender? Surrender requires obedience, and it is this obedience that turns into our acts of worship. We need to know that worshipping God brings His blessings. We must not *use* obedience and surrender and worship as a means to receive His blessings. God can only bless the true love in our hearts that allows us to worship. We must have truthful and honest obedience and worship to be blessed by Him. The blessings are as He sees fit and in His timing.

Importantly too, our worship must cost us something; it cannot be worthless. Think of Abraham, whose obedience would have cost him his son, Isaac. Recall Genesis 22:15–18: *"Then the Angel of the Lord called to Abraham a second time out of heaven, and said: 'By Myself I have sworn,' says the Lord, 'because you have done this thing, and have not withheld your son, your only son—blessing I will bless you, and multiplying I will multiply your descendants as the stars of the heaven and as the sand which is on the seashore; and your descendants shall possess the gate of their enemies. In your seed all the nations of the earth shall be blessed, because you have obeyed My voice.'"*

I can say with confidence that God isn't going to ask us to sacrifice our children the way Abraham was told to. But God does ask us to do things. He asks us to witness, to speak, or to stand up for Him and for others. He asks us to use our gifts, to forgive, to help, to give our time and money and energy to others. How obedient are we to those nudges, the requests we know come from Him? These things come with a cost. Time, energy, and emotion have a cost to us. Finances have a cost to us. It *all* costs us something. This obedience is a true act of worship that we cannot shrug off or minimize. It builds the Kingdom. It heals the Kingdom. And it goes straight to the heart of the Creator, who loves us dearly.

We are called to worship. We are made for it. I have found that worship enables me to do more for Him, because in the pouring out of my heart to Him, I am filled with more of Him. Worship is like going to the gym; it strengthens muscles of faith and obedience and surrender, all key ingredients in a victorious life. Memorizing scripture is also a form of worship. Anything that lets us say and live the words "Lord, Your will be done" is worship. Cultivate a worshipping heart, mind, and life, and God's blessings will flow your way. This is also why worship and praise are weapons of war—weapons to us warriors who fight every day in and for our faith. The enemy is always looking for ways to steal our joy and remove our opportunity to give worship to God. It is so important to know the value of worshipping, especially when we feel as if we have hit a wall.

Matthew 6:33 says, *"But seek ye first the kingdom of God and His righteousness, and all these things shall be added to you."* When we position ourselves in His presence, the outcome can only be amazing. Every single person is wired for and meant to worship. If you have a beating heart, you were made for worship. Worship is not based on talent but on *heart*.

A Sinful Woman Forgiven

My favourite story about worship is about the sinful woman at the Pharisee's house, in Luke 7:36–39. *"Then one of the Pharisees asked Him to eat with him. And He went to the Pharisee's house and sat down to eat. And behold, a woman in the city who was a sinner, when she knew that Jesus sat at the table in the Pharisee's house, brought an alabaster flask of fragrant oil, and stood at His feet behind Him weeping; and she began to wash His feet with her tears, and wiped them with the hair of her head; and she kissed His feet and anointed them with the fragrant oil. Now when the Pharisee who had invited Him saw this, he spoke to himself, saying, 'This Man, if He were a prophet, would know who and what manner of woman this is who is touching Him, for she is a sinner.'"*

Everything we learned about God so far—His names, His promises, His love, and His tender mercy—brings us to this point: worship. Our hearts fill with love and awe, and we are moved to do something about it. The wonder is not just at what God does, but more about who God is. This woman worshipped Jesus for who He was. Simple. Pure. True. What I love about her is that she brought *all she had*. She yielded her *will and pride*. She stood in the face of *opposition*. Being there *cost her something*. She expressed her heart of love *honestly* and *freely*.

We should all take note of her. Jesus dignified her. He let her leave in peace and forgiveness (she received His blessings). Her worship was an expression of her faith *before* Jesus did anything for her. She didn't wait until afterwards to praise Him. She worshipped Him because of Who He was, not because of what He did. We can also learn from her to not be too concerned with what people think about us, whenever or wherever we worship. Just bring it. Give it. Let it flow from you to the Creator and let the magic into your life.

CPSIA information can be obtained
at www.ICGtesting.com
Printed in the USA
LVHW092007080419
613436LV00001B/2/P